DRUGS OF ABUSE
From Doctors to Dealers, Users and Healers

Informative • Concise • Illustrated • Historical

Michael Palladini, RPh, MBA

Three Suns Publishing
516 College Avenue
Beaver, PA 15009

Contact: info@drugsofabuse.net
Designed by Brkich Design (www.brkichdesign.com)

ISBN-13 978-0-9835914-0-5

*This book is dedicated to my wife Erin,
and my three sons Michael, Noah and John.*

Table of Contents

Preface...3

Introduction...5

Pharmacology...7

   NOMENCLATURE...8
   DRUG FORMS...8
   DRUG ROUTES 10
   EFFECTS 11
   DRUG ACTION 12
   CHRONIC DRUG ACTION 14
   PHARMACOKINETICS 15
   NEUROTRANSMITTERS 20

Opiates 25

   HISTORY OF OPIATES...27
   EFFECTS AND ACTIONS 33
   NATURAL OPIATES 34
      Opium, Morphine, Codeine 34
   SEMISYNTHETIC OPIATES...................................38
      Heroin, Oxymorphone, Oxycodone,
      Hydromorphone, Hydrocodone, Buprenorphine 38
   SYNTHETIC OPIATES...48
      Fentanyl, Meperidine, Methadone................................48
   MISCELLANEOUS OPIATES..................................53
      Propoxyphene, Tramadol 53
   APPENDIX 1 123
      Opiate Products
      Pharmacokinetic Profiles of the Opiates
      Opiate Withdrawal Profile

Stimulants..55

   EFFECTS AND ACTIONS 56
   COCAINE..57
      History of Cocaine...57
   FORMS AND USE..59
   AMPHETAMINES 63
      History of Amphetamines...............................63
      Methamphetamine 66

METHYLPHENIDATE 69

ANORECTICS..70

KHAT...74

APPENDIX 2...129
Amphetamine Products
Methylphenidate Products

Depressants 77

HISTORY OF BARBITURATES AND BENZODIAZEPINES.....................78

BARBITURATES 79

BENZODIAZEPINES 82
Action, Effects, Tolerance, Withdrawal 84

BENZODIAZEPINE PRODUCTS..86
Alprazolam, Chlordiazepoxide, Clonazepam, Clorazepate,
Diazepam, Estazolam, Flurazepam, Lorazepam, Midazolam,
Oxazepam,Temazepam, Triazolam 87

FLUNITRAZEPAM..92

ZOLPIDEM 93

GHB 94

QUETIAPINE...95

CARISOPRODOL 96

APPENDIX 3...133
Barbiturate Products
Benzodiazepine Products

Hallucinogens 99

NATURAL HALLUCINOGENS..100
Cannabis, Mescaline, Psilocybin 100

SYNTHETIC HALLUCINOGENS 107
LSD, MDMA, PCP, Ketamine, Dextromethorphan...........................107

MISCELLANEOUS HALLUCINOGENS 116

APPENDIX 4...141
Controlled Substance Act, Schedules
Drug Use Timetable

Case Studies 117

Bibliography...143

Preface

The human mind has always intrigued me. As a young psychology student, I learned of the complexity of our brain and the vast amount of information processed, interpreted and stored by this amazing part of our body. While studying pharmacy, the drugs that affect the brain became increasingly interesting to me, as they seemed powerful chemicals, capable of changing moods, perceptions, and ultimately transforming lives. During the past 20 years that I have been associated with pharmacy, the medical community began using drugs as never before to treat diagnoses of anxiety, depression, insomnia and pain, to name a few. Drug use escalated, from doctor offices to clinics, from television advertisements to the street corner. A drug culture was forming in the many corners of our society that has led to the social epidemic that we are currently facing.

I have also had the unique opportunity of working with many individuals whose lives have been afflicted by drug use, and the professionals who work in the drug treatment field. My time spent over several years as a drug and alcohol counselor, facilitator and educator has allowed me access into these lives, and has helped me to develop a new direction in my own career. The many stories of these people has led me to determine the best possible way that I could contribute to this vital arena, which seemed a combination of the bodies of knowledge that I had made my own life's work.

The book that you hold in your hands is the product of my efforts, a guide to assist the many individuals whose lives have somehow become touched by the drug culture. I would like to thank the many people who have allowed me to become a part of their recovery, a part of their career, and who have helped me to realize a rewarding and worthwhile effort.

– Mike Palladini

Introduction

Drug abuse has become quite the household word. Prescription drug abuse is now more common in the U.S. than illegal drug abuse, as prescription medication is found in many places other than the bottle from the pharmacy. Celebrities make news with abuse problems, doctors make news with prescribing issues, and children prefer pain pills to alcohol and cigarettes. These trends all amount to a need for "mainstreaming" education about drugs of abuse, as the misuse of substances has certainly caught the general attention of the public and the media, and does not seem to be going away.

"Drugs of Abuse: From Doctors to Dealers, Users and Healers" was written in an attempt to inform all of these groups involved with drug use, from doctors who prescribe to users who may begin to misuse. Many involved with caring for others, in the healthcare field, in our schools, and in our homes, must improve their understanding of the drugs being abused on the street and in our institutions. Parents must be informed of the substances to which their children are being exposed, if prevention and education about the misuse of drugs is to be successful.

The contents of this book will present drugs of abuse within general categories, noting effects of the drugs on those under the influence, as well as street names and prices, and numerous images of the drugs. Historical information is provided to allow the reader to grasp the impact that many of these drugs have had on our society, and the ongoing problems that have occurred.

For anyone with an interest professionally or personally in drugs and medications, this book will serve as both a reference source and an educating journey into drug use in our society. "Mainstreaming" education to match the mainstream use of these drugs today will place those informed in a better position to understand the challenges associated with drugs of abuse.

The material in this book has been obtained from federal agency postings and reports, numerous textbooks and articles, and hours of personal interviews with patients in recovery from substance abuse.

Pharmacology

Why does morphine affect one person in a particular way, but another person differently? How long does a drug actually stay in a person's body? Why does snorting a drug affect a person differently than swallowing a pill? These questions are answered in terms of pharmacology, which is the study of drugs and their actions and effects in living systems. Pharmacology is involved with all drugs, including legal, illegal, prescription, and over-the-counter medications.

Dosages and frequency of administering, routes of administration, length of time in the body, and adverse side effects are all areas that are addressed by the study of pharmacology.

The purpose of this book is to present the drugs of abuse within the major categories of opiates, stimulants, depressants, and hallucinogens. A better understanding of pharmacology is an important introduction to these drugs, as well as developing the terminology necessary for a discussion rooted in chemical and pharmaceutical language. Heroin, cocaine, methamphetamine, marijuana, oxycodone are all chemicals; chemicals that are used as drugs. Let's talk about them chemically, as well as socially, to better understand what these drugs of abuse truly are.

Nomenclature

Drugs are named in several different ways. All drugs will have a "chemical name," which is the actual description of the drug based on its chemical composition. There is also a "generic name," which could also be the chemical name, but usually an abbreviated version of the lengthy chemical name for convenience. Finally, there is the "trade" or "brand" name of the drug, a proprietary trademark of the chemical by the manufacturer.

For example, the "chemical name" of 2-acetoxybenzoic acid is also referred to as the "generic name" of acetylsalicylic acid or the "trade name" aspirin. The pain reliever marketed as Vicodin also goes by the generic name hydrocodone, but is rarely referred to by its chemical name of 4,5a-Epoxy-3-methoxy-17-methylmorphinan-6-one. It is important to recognize that a drug may be called by either a brand name or generic name, but that it is indeed the same chemical.

Drug Forms

Many drugs are available in different forms, or formulations. Pharmaceutics is the science of formulating drugs into different types of preparations for use in the best possible manner, such as tablets, capsules, ointments, or injectables. A capsule may be easier to swallow than a tablet, or an injectable may produce an effect faster than a tablet taken by mouth. Liquid forms of drugs are available for younger and older patients unable to swallow a tablet or capsule. A patient's condition may prevent medication from being used in the stomach; therefore, an injectable form is used in order to bypass the stomach. There are many considerations, both relating to the patient and the chemical nature of the drug, which rely on the availability of different dosage forms to deliver the medication.

Solid drugs consist of tablets and capsules, commonly referred to as "pills."

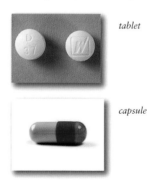

tablet

capsule

A tablet or capsule may be designed to dissolve in the stomach and release its entire contents all at once, which is termed an "immediate release" form of the drug. Often, tablets or capsules are designed to dissolve slowly after being taken, either by incorporating a coating on the tablet, a series of layers in the tablet, or slow-release "beads" of medicine within the capsule.

This helps to achieve the goal of delivering medication to a patient for an extended period of time, allowing for fewer doses throughout the day, and less likelihood of forgetting or missing a dose of medication. Medications of this type of formulation are named extended-release, sustained-release, time-release, or delayed-release, and may include the initials XR, SR, XL in their name. If the coating or built-in mechanism of the manufactured drug were broken, then the entire amount of drug designed for 12 or 24 hours worth of medication is released at one time. This can be simply done by crushing or chewing a tablet or capsule. For example, an Oxycontin® 80mg tablet, a pain reliever meant to deliver 80mg of medication for 12 hours of relief, may be chewed or crushed to get all 80mg of the drug at one time.

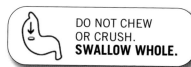

Liquid drug forms are available as syrups, solutions, suspensions, elixirs and tinctures. Slight differences in the manner in which the medication, or solid drug, is dissolved into solution determines the form of the liquid. Syrups are solutions that contain sugar for sweetness. Solutions are a solid or liquid form of the drug dissolved into another liquid, and may also be elixirs or tinctures. An elixir is a liquid that contains water, alcohol and sugar. A tincture is solely an alcohol preparation of the drug. A suspension is a solid drug form that is not completely dissolved in a liquid, but rather "suspended" in it. This type of form requires shaking prior to using to mix the contents together.

In addition to oral dosage forms such as tablets and liquids, there are injectable and

topical forms of drugs. Injectables allow for rapid administration of a drug directly into the blood stream (intravenous, or IV) and into the muscle (intramuscular, or IM), or just under the skin (subcutaneously, or SC).

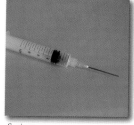

Injectable drug

Syringe

Transdermal patches

Topical drug forms include transdermal patches that are applied to the skin for absorption of medication through the skin and into the bloodstream. Most medications manufactured as a transdermal delivery system or patch are intended to be worn for an extended period of time and eliminate the need for repeated oral or injectable doses of the drug. Again, the manufactured mechanism for allowing a slow, extended release of the drug can be bypassed by ripping or tearing the patch and destroying the barrier that controls the release of the drug.

Drug Routes

Medications in different forms may be delivered to the body by different methods. The drug forms discussed, such as tablets and injectables, are obviously meant to be used in a variety of ways. These methods of administration are called *routes*. Taking a tablet by mouth is the *oral* route of administration. A patch applied to the skin is the *transdermal* route of administration. An injection into a vein is called the *intravenous* or IV route of administration. There are other routes of administration, which are summarized in the following table. Each route of administration has an associated *onset of action,* which refers to the length of time that it takes for the drug to be absorbed into the bloodstream and to have an effect in the body. It would be expected that an intravenous injection, for example, injected directly into the bloodstream, would have a faster onset of action than a tablet taken by mouth, as the tablet would need to dissolve in the stomach and then be absorbed through various tissues in the gastrointestinal tract.

ROUTES OF ADMINISTRATION

ROUTE (Abbreviation)	DESCRIPTION	APPROXIMATE ONSET OF ACTION
Oral (PO)	By mouth	30 to 60 minutes
Sublingual (SL)	Under the tongue	Several minutes
Buccal	Between the cheek and gum	Several minutes
Rectal	In the rectum	15 to 30 minutes
Transdermal	On the skin	30 to 60 minutes
Subcutaneous (SC)	Injected just below the skin	Several minutes
Intramuscular (IM)	Injected into a muscle	Several minutes
Intravenous (IV)	Injected into a vein	Within 1 minute
Inhalation	Inhaled into the lungs	Within 1 minute
Topical	Applied onto a skin surface	Within 1 hour
Vaginal	Into the vagina	15 to 30 minutes

Notice that IV injection can produce an onset of action within 1 minute. The inhalation route directly into the lungs (smoking) produces the same results, with effects felt by the drug user within one minute. Remember that the onset of action is determined by the drug entering the bloodstream and reaching the area of the body where it can be effective, known as the target site. The lungs are filled with small air sacs called alveoli, which come in contact with many blood capillaries, allowing for fast entrance of an inhaled drug into the bloodstream. It has been said that the surface area of the human lungs, if unfolded and flattened, would be the size of a football field. With the brain being the target area of many drugs of abuse, the effects of the drug are felt very quickly through inhaling, similar to injecting IV. Thus the popularity of smoking cocaine (crack), opium, nicotine (cigarettes), and marijuana. If a drug is not broken down by heat and remains stable in the vapor, then it can be smoked and its effects felt by the brain very quickly. Onset of action is a vital component of a drug profile when considering drugs that are abused, as the immediate effects of the drug on the brain are what are sought after by the abuser. The intensified effects of the drug that produce the associated euphoria must be obtained by the fastest route of onset as possible. Concentrating the drug and making it available to certain areas of the brain quickly are what create the euphoric and desired effects.

Effects

Since a drug is basically a chemical, with chemical properties that act on the human body at the cellular level, the drug is going to have certain effects on the body. These effects may be desired or *therapeutic* effects, or they may be undesired or side effects. Most drugs will create *side* effects in the user, and are mainly considered being more a nuisance than harmful. These effects include dry mouth, nausea, sedation, constipation, and so forth. An adverse effect is also an undesired effect, but may be more harmful to the user, and may create conditions that would justify stopping the drug. This would include mental confusion, severe nausea, or any condition that would involve a major organ such as the kidney or liver. A toxic effect would be drug poisoning, and could have harmful or life-threatening consequences. The drug must be stopped immediately and additional medical care may be necessary. A drug overdose would be an example of a toxic effect.

"Only the dose separates a drug from a poison" – Paracelsus (1493-1541)

Even in the Middle Ages, the toxic effects of drugs were apparent, as Paracelsus, a physician at the time, made that famous statement. A small amount of a certain drug may produce the desired effect, but only a small amount more may become toxic. The dose is the amount of the drug taken at one time. Manufacturers, prescribers, and those who dispense and administer drugs are familiar with the proper doses of the drugs being used.

Drug Action

Once a drug is administered, it must do what it is intended to do. We take an aspirin for a headache, or a sedative to relax. One uses amphetamines for alertness, and LSD for a mind-altering experience. All of these drugs have a particular intended action for their use, and a particular part of the body where they are effective. The mechanism of action of a drug explains how a drug produces its effects. Aspirin reduces inflammation by interfering with certain enzymes in the body that create chemicals that lead to inflammation. Sedatives increase certain neurotransmitters in the brain that have a calming or sedating effect. The site of action of a drug is the location in the body where the drug has its main therapeutic effect. For most of the drugs of abuse, the brain is the site of action, although side effects occur in various other sites.

Once a drug reaches the site of action in the body, it exerts its effects chemically at the cellular level. The drug must enter the cell or attach to the cell to have the appropriate effect, which results in a complex chemical reaction. There seems to be certain areas on the cell that drugs attach to more easily than other areas. These areas are known as receptor sites, and these specific sites are known and identified on cells for specific drugs. For example, morphine and all of the opiate drugs, attach to a specific area of certain cells in the brain and other areas of the body to produce their effects. The opiate receptor sites are known as *mu receptors,* named after the Greek letter for M, referring to morphine. There are many receptor sites identified throughout the human body, in various tissue and organ systems, which relate to cellular activity between drugs and the cells of those particular systems.

Imagine a cell surface that is like a lock, and a drug that is a key.

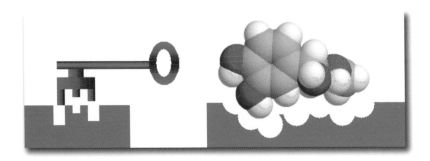

The cell "accepts" the drug by a specific chemical fit that initiates the chemical reaction that follows and produces the effects of the drug on the cell. The chemical composition of the drug is illustrated as a "shape" that matches the surface of the cell. This can be depicted by the following simplified diagram of the opiate receptor,

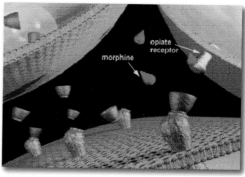

which is receptive to the drug morphine:

Another way of looking at the cell receptor activity is to compare the following two photographs:

A dog's nose has many more surface cells that are sensitive to chemicals than the human nose. These cells can "accept" and recognize many different chemicals associated with smell. Similarly, different cells in the human body have many more surface receptor sites than other cells, and therefore "accept" or react with certain chemicals more readily.

There are many different types of receptor sites on the many different types of cells in the human body. Drugs react differently with these receptor sites based on their chemical composition. Again, the "lock and key" concept. A drug that reacts with a receptor site and produces an effect is called an *agonist* drug. There are drugs that react, or bind with a receptor site and produce no effect, as if they were blocking the site. These drugs are called *antagonist* drugs. Drugs will compete with each other for available receptor sites when in the body together. Some drugs have a stronger chemical attraction for the receptor than other drugs. This helps to explain drug interactions that cause one drug to lose effectiveness when a second drug is administered.

Chronic Drug Action

Extensive, long term drug use is called chronic drug use, and chronic drug action effects result in changes to a person's response to the drug, both pharmacologically and physiologically. As the receptor sites on the cells continue to interact and bind with the drug time after time, day after day, and perhaps months into years, the cell becomes unable to interact properly with the drug. It becomes "desensitized" to the drug and begins to require more and more of the drug to produce the same effects. This is called drug tolerance, and is defined as a decreased effect of a drug after repeated administration. Drug tolerance may develop very quickly, perhaps only after several weeks, or may take much longer. The inability of the cell surface to produce adequate receptor sites to accommodate the ongoing large amounts of drug results in a reduction of the intensity of the drug's effect. This activity is referred to as "down- regulation," where the actual number of receptors decreases due to chronic activation. There also exists "up-regulation" where the number of receptors will increase and cause more sensitivity to a drug.

Chronic drug use results in a decreased response to the drug due to the cell receptor becoming "desensitized," or the decreased number of receptors available. This condition is known as tolerance, which is defined as the need for increasing amounts of a drug to produce the same effect. *Tolerance* to a drug many occur rapidly, after long periods of chronic use, or never. Tolerance to a drug is reversible when use of the drug stops, therefore, the effects of the drug may be experienced at the original dosage. To illustrate an example of tolerance related to chronic drug use, a chronic heroin user may use as much as 2 grams of heroin without consequence, while the lethal dose for a novice user may be as low as 200mg.

The condition that results from chronic drug use and the reliance on that drug to maintain a state of well-being is called drug dependence. *Dependence* is characterized as being either physical and/or psychological. Drugs of abuse all have some degree of psychological dependence, wherein the user feels an overpowering need and desire to use the drug. Physical dependence relates to the symptoms experienced when the drug is not taken, known as withdrawal symptoms. These are unpleasant, measurable changes in body functions, such as diarrhea, insomnia, muscle aches, which occur as the body attempts to adjust to functionality without the drug's presence.

Pharmacokinetics

As we have seen, a drug may be taken in various forms and by different routes of administration. The drug must bind with receptors on cells in different parts of the body to have its intended effect, as well as some unintended side effects. The drug does not exert its effect indefinitely, as it leaves the receptor site and is eventually rendered useless in the body, and removed. All of these processes are considered by the study of pharmacokinetics, the activity of a drug in the body over an extended period of time.

Pharmacokinetics is broken down into four processes of drug activity:

1. Absorption
2. Distribution
3. Metabolism
4. Elimination

Each of these areas defines a particular process along the pathway of a drug throughout the human body.

Drug Absorption

The initial pharmacokinetic process is absorption, which refers to the entrance of the drug into the bloodstream. A drug taken orally must dissolve in the stomach or the small intestine before it can be absorbed by the body into the bloodstream. To achieve this, it must pass through the lining of the stomach or small intestine and pass into the bloodstream. Many factors can affect the extent and rate of absorption, and must be considered to assure that an optimal amount of drug reaches the intended part of the body. The drug form will affect the rate of absorption, as a tablet must dissolve before it can be absorbed, whereas a liquid medication does not, and will absorb faster. IV (intravenous) drug forms enter the bloodstream immediately and will bypass the stomach entirely, achieving a faster rate of absorption. The same is true for inhaled medications through the lungs, transdermal patches, and IM (intramuscular) injections. The lining of the stomach and small intestines, referred to as the gastrointestinal (GI) tract, are made of fats (lipids) and proteins. To dissolve through the lining easily and reach the bloodstream, a drug must have a similar chemical makeup. The saying is "like dissolves like," meaning that, chemically speaking, a drug will dissolve into another substance if it is a similar type of chemical. Drugs with a high lipid molecular content will dissolve through the GI lining more easily, and reach the bloodstream better and faster. Other factors that affect the rate and extent of drug absorption are the pH of the stomach, and the presence of food in the stomach. An additional consideration with oral absorption of drugs is something called the "first-pass effect," which refers to the fact that drugs taken orally will pass through the liver first before entering the general bloodstream, and may be broken down considerably. This process will be discussed in the metabolism section, but affects the absorption of orally taken drugs.

Drug Distribution

The absorbed drug now moves into the bloodstream and further into other tissues and organs of the body, and ultimately to its intended site of action. This process is known as distribution. The main factor affecting the distribution of a drug is blood flow, as various organs and areas of the body receive more blood than others. The liver, brain, and kidneys have the largest blood supply, and are thus exposed to the largest amount of drug. Adipose (fat) tissue does not have much of a blood supply and therefore does not receive much absorbed drug. However, as discussed earlier, some highly fat-soluble drugs may reach fat deposits, dissolve, accumulate and remain there.

The blood is full of chemicals called proteins, and drugs in the bloodstream will bind with these proteins through chemical processes and become "tied-up" and unavailable for use in other body tissue. Some drugs experience 99% protein binding, and this activity must be accounted for when formulating drug dosages. Thus, there is unbound or "free" drug available or "protein-bound" drug unavailable. Drug manufacturers design drug doses to compensate for the degree of protein binding that a particular drug exhibits.

The intended site of action of many of the drugs of abuse is the brain. Surrounding the brain is an additional layer of lipid cells that form a protective membrane, called the blood brain barrier. This membrane prevents many substances from entering the brain through the large supply of blood that the brain receives.

Nutrients may pass through the membrane to the brain cells, such as water, oxygen and glucose. Since the blood brain barrier is made of lipid cells, highly lipid-soluble drugs ("like dissolves like") pass through into the brain easily. For example, the fat-soluble drug heroin enters the brain and exerts its effect more easily and more quickly than the drug morphine, which is more water-soluble.

Drug Metabolism

A drug is considered a foreign substance inside the body, and thus the body attempts to eliminate it through different processes. Some drugs are excreted unchanged by the body, leaving the system in exactly the same form in which they entered. Most drugs, however, are chemically altered throughout their journey in the body, and must be additionally altered before they can be eliminated. This process of chemically altering drugs and other foreign substances in the body is called metabolism. The organ responsible for this process is the liver, which contains cells that produce enzymes, chemicals that initiate and carry-out the alteration process. Simply stated, these enzymes take lipid-soluble chemicals, which, as has been discussed, are more chemically active and more easily absorbed in tissues throughout the body, and alter them to be more water-soluble. Water soluble chemicals or drugs are more easily excreted by the kidneys.

The enzymes produced in the liver attack drugs in different manners, depending on the chemistry of the drug, and the necessary reaction needed to create a water-soluble chemical for excretion. The activity level of these enzymes determines the extent and rate of metabolism of drugs, and the ultimate amount of drug available to the body. As mentioned earlier, the first-pass effect involves orally administered drugs that pass into the bloodstream and through the liver before reaching the target sites of action, and are subject to enzyme degradation prior to doing anything, thus reducing overall drug bioavailability.

Other factors that affect metabolism and liver enzyme levels are age, disease states, and genetic disposition. Certain drugs, when given together, may attract the same enzymes for metabolism, and affect the degradation rate of one or the other competitively. Other drugs may stimulate the liver to produce even more enzymes, thus affecting the metabolism of other drugs in the body. Nicotine (smoking), phenobarbital, and Tagamet® are examples of these enzyme-inducing drugs.

Drug Elimination
The last stage of pharmacokinetics involves excretion, or removal of the drug from the body. This process is referred to as elimination, and the route is through the kidneys. As the drug has been made water-soluble by the enzyme activity of the liver, it is now able to pass from the bloodstream and into the kidney for filtration out of the body. The drug is now rendered into a form that is useless in the body and is considered waste for removal.

Other routes of excretion of drug from the body include the lungs, sweat, saliva, and breast milk. Alcohol is excreted through the lungs, while aspirin and the barbiturates are known to be excreted through breast milk.

Additional Pharmacology
There are a few additional topics and terms to become familiar with before ending
a discussion on pharmacology. This information has been presented in a format
that is intended as an introduction, and is not intended to be exhaustive or
extremely detailed. The terminology and processes have been included to help in a
greater understanding of drug behavior in general, which can be extended to a
discussion of drugs of abuse. After all, drugs of abuse are abused for their effects,
which is a pharmacological term.

Dose-Response Curve
A dose response curve illustrates the fact that the greater a dose that is given, the
greater the response experienced. Eventually, however, the response will reach a
high point where no further therapeutic response is possible, regardless of how
much additional drug is given. Side effects or adverse effects may increase, but the
cell receptors responsible for the intended clinical therapeutic effect are saturated
and unable to provide any further drug action.

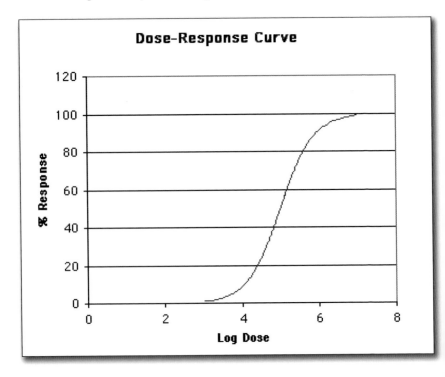

Where the response reaches 100%, or the height of response curve, is called the ceiling and the inability for any further response is called the ceiling effect. Many users of drugs of abuse attempt to break the ceiling of the response curve in vain by increasing the dosage taken, unknowingly increasing the likelihood of only toxic effects.

Duration of Action

A drug experiences the pharmacokinetic processes as it travels from site of administration to final elimination. At any point in time, the drug will be in the bloodstream at various "levels" or amounts. Due to the variations in absorption, distribution, metabolism and elimination, all processes occurring simultaneously, the drug levels in the bloodstream will change as time passes. The amount of time that the drug exists in its active form in the bloodstream is called its duration of action, and may be several minutes to many hours in length. The lowest level of drug that is determined in the bloodstream is the trough and the highest level is the peak.

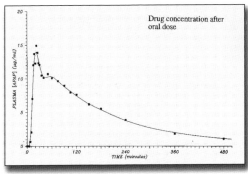

Duration of Action curve

Drug half-life

The time required for a drug to be eliminated from the body is expressed by a term called drug half-life. This is the time necessary for the body to eliminate half of the drug. All drugs have their respective half-lives. For example, the half-life of codeine is 3 hours, meaning that every 3 hours half of the amount of available codeine is eliminated from the body. A longer drug half-life corresponds to a longer duration of action of the drug. (Fentanyl has a half-life closer to 7 hours, and thus a longer duration of action than codeine). Five to seven "half-lives" of time will

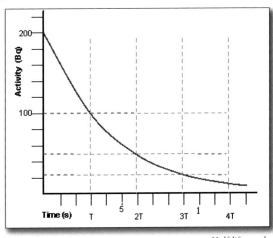

Half-life graph

lead to a level of less than 3% of drug in the bloodstream, and is considered eliminated. Therefore, codeine with a half-life of 3 hours will be effectively eliminated from the body in 15 to 21 hours, provided no additional drug is taken. Fentanyl will be eliminated in 35 to 49 hours.

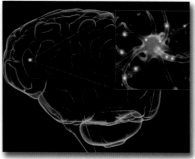

Nerve cell and neurotransmitters

Neurotransmitters

The principal target site of drugs of abuse is the central nervous system, especially the brain. The brain is made up of millions of nerve cells, which utilize a combination of electrical signaling and a chemical messenger mechanism to process information.

When stimulated by a receptor on the cell body, the electrical process diagrammed begins and travels at speeds of up to 200 miles per hour, going from one neuron to the next until a target in the brain is reached. The networks of neurons in the brain interact and "consult" with each other, and ultimately create a result. Within this extremely complex network of millions of nerve cells, the ends of individual neurons amazingly do not touch another neuron, but terminate in a microscopic gap called a synapse. The synaptic gap between two neurons is approximately 20 nanometers wide. A nanometer is a very small distance. One-hundred thousand nanometers would fit across a human hair.

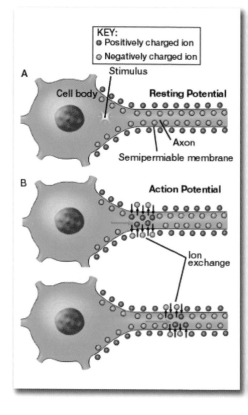

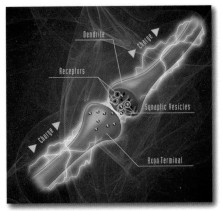

So what happens to the electrical charge that is travelling through the nerve cell to stimulate other nerve cells and ultimately process information or produce a response? It was originally thought that the electrical charge jumped the synaptic gap and moved on, but it was determined that a chemical was stimulated at the end of one nerve cell and "crossed the gap" to the next. These chemicals are known as neurotransmitters, and are vital to the functioning of the brain in humans.

These neurotransmitters cross the synapse at 1,000 times per second, carrying on the message through to the next neuron and throughout the brain.

Neurotransmitters in the brain are the substances that are affected by the drugs of abuse, as the drugs will enhance, block or mimic the natural effects of these chemical messengers.

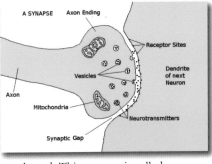

The neurotransmitter's life in the synapse is very brief, as the nervous system "recycles" these chemicals by built-in mechanisms that draw them back into the neuron from which they were released. This process is called reuptake, and ensures that the neurotransmitters exert their effect briefly and are available for the next transmission. A finely tuned chemical balance is maintained. Many drugs act by blocking this reuptake process, and thus create an overabundance of neurotransmitters in the synapse and an increased effect on the receiving cell receptors. These drugs are called reuptake inhibitors and are used for depression and other disease states. Drugs of abuse, for example cocaine, work by blocking the reuptake of neurotransmitters and creating a flood of these chemical messengers in the synapses of the brain nerve cells.

Within the brain are certain areas that are responsible for functions such as heartbeat, breathing, body temperature, digestion, as well as emotions and cravings (anger, fear, hunger, thirst, sex, pleasure). As certain areas of the brain are stimulated by outside influences, the neurotransmitters involved in the processing of information in the brain will affect the emotion, reward or pleasure centers, but will also affect the areas responsible for the basic body functions described as well. The reward/pleasure center of the brain is connected very closely with the network of brain cells that regulate the body functions. Therefore, a drug that is taken for pleasure will also create unwanted side effects due to stimulation of the neurotransmitters in the areas of the brain that control those basic body functions also.

Below is a listing of the major neurotransmitters and their areas of function, as well as the associated drugs of abuse.

Major Neurotransmitters

ACETYLCHOLINE – arousal/reward/sensory perceptions
Nicotine: Increases release

NOREPINEPHRINE – attention/focus/depression
Amphetamine: Increases levels by preventing reuptake

DOPAMINE – sleep/mood/attention/memory/reward
Cocaine: Increase levels by preventing reuptake

GABA – inhibition/"decrease cell activity"
Benzodiazepine: Increase levels

SEROTONIN – mood/sexuality/sleep
Hallucinogens: Impairs reuptake

ENDORPHIN – well-being
Opiates: mimics receptor binding

This is, of course, a very simplified list of the neurotransmitters and their respective functions. But it will serve as a focal point when discussing the effects of the drugs of abuse on the brain and body systems. The drugs of abuse will either mimic and exaggerate or block the effects of neurotransmitters to achieve their desired effect. Most drugs will affect more than one neurotransmitter and will cause multiple effects in the user. An example would be the cocaine user who enjoys the euphoric rush of the drug entering the brain and causing a huge imbalance of the neurotransmitters dopamine, serotonin and norepinephrine. The drug blocks the nerve cell's natural tendency to remove the neurotransmitters after they are used, thus they "build-up" in the synaptic gap and continue to have an exaggerated effect. The increased serotonin levels would lead to increased feelings of pleasure and confidence, while the high levels of norepinephrine would cause increased heart rate, breathing and energy. The euphoria associated with cocaine use is related to the amplified levels of dopamine that the affected nerve cells pump out due to activation by the cocaine chemical.

The interaction of drugs of abuse and nerve cells and the neurotransmitters is what determines the effects that these drugs have on the user. The human brain is a complex network of cells, chemicals and electrical energy in a biochemical balance. The inclusion of drugs, especially chronically and at high levels, will disrupt this finely tuned balance and create effects that are interpreted as being euphoric and dreamlike, or painful and nightmarish.

Opiates

Narcotics. Pain relievers. Analgesics. The opiates are known by many names, including the broad categories listed here. All opiates, or *opioids* as they are also called, meaning "like opiate," are derived from the opium plant. The sap of the immature seed pod of the opium plant contains a latex mix of sugars, proteins, fats, and other substances, including the alkaloids morphine and codeine. An *alkaloid* is a term for a naturally occurring chemical compound.

The opium poppy plant

The opiates relieve pain, and for this reason the prescription drugs that are known as painkillers have become very commonly used by doctors. Opiate painkillers are also used to treat a severe cough or diarrhea, as the effects of opiate drugs are experienced in an area of the brain known as the cough center, and in the gastrointestinal system. The effects of the opiates are experienced by the drug user as pain relief, sedation, relaxation, and euphoria. It is these effects that the opiates produce that make them effective drugs, yet highly abused.

Within the opium latex sap, the opium plant produces three naturally occurring alkaloids which are used as drugs themselves or chemicals to form other drugs. These three naturally occurring alkaloids are morphine, codeine, and thebaine. Morphine and codeine are used as drugs, or are chemically altered to create other narcotics, known as *semi-synthetic narcotics*. The thebaine alkaloid does not have any drug activity itself, but is used to chemically create *semi-synthetic narcotics* as well.

The *semi-synthetic narcotics* include the drugs heroin, hydromorphone, oxymorphone, oxycodone, hydrocodone, and buprenorphine. These drugs are chemically altered versions of the naturally occurring morphine, codeine, and thebaine to produce drugs that have increased potency and duration of action, and less side effects.

There also exist completely synthetic narcotics that have been produced to provide long acting drugs with specialized goals in treating patients. The synthetic narcotics include methadone, meperidine, and fentanyl.

The opiate products can be seen in appendix 1.

The many available opiates, or narcotics, on the market allow for a variety of different drugs in numerous forms that a prescribing physician has at his disposal to treat a patient in pain. The natural or synthetic nature of the drugs offers varying strengths, duration of action, or ability to administer orally or intravenously (IV). The specific characteristics of each drug allow a physician to select the most appropriate narcotic for that patient's complaints. The many different available opiates also tend to offer an increasing number of options for those seeking the euphoric effects or nonmedical use of these drugs. As will be discussed, the opioid drugs have many similar characteristics and produce similar effects in the user, but the differences among the drugs create a greater potential for abuse and dependence on the drug. These differences and similarities will hopefully become clearer as the opiates are viewed from a historical perspective, as well as chemically and pharmacologically.

The History of Opiates

"Among the remedies which it has pleased Almighty God to give to man to relieve his sufferings, none is so universal and so efficacious as opium."
–Thomas Sydenham, 17th century pioneer in English medicine

"I'll die young, but it's like kissing God"
–Lenny Bruce (speaking of heroin)

Papaver somniferum, the opium poppy, can be traced through archaeological evidence and fossilized seeds to the ancient civilizations of Persia, Egypt, and Mesopotamia to around the time 4000 BC. It was referred to as *Hul Gil,* the *"joy plant."* Poppy images appear in Egyptian pictography and Roman sculpture, and opium containing preparations were enjoyed as remedies for many illnesses throughout these areas for centuries.

The use of opium spread to Arabia, India and China by traders and warriors. During this time, opium was ground up and eaten, or mixed with water. The Greek physician Galen listed the medical indications of opium as curing "chronic headache, vertigo, asthma, cough, spitting of blood, tightness of breath, colic, fever, melancholy, and all pestilences."

During the early part of the sixteenth century, approximately 1527 AD, the European chemist known as Paracelsus dissolved opium in brandy. The alkaloids found in opium are not very soluble in water, and are not extracted very well from the opium compound when simply dissolved in water or eaten. However, the alkaloids are significantly more soluble in alcohol, and when dissolved in alcohol, create a *tincture* with a much higher potency. Paracelsus called this tincture *laudanum* meaning "something to be praised." The use of laudanum became very popular throughout Europe during the seventeenth century, being recommended by physicians of the time for pain, sleeplessness, and diarrhea. The use of opium as laudanum was considered a cure-all, and became the basis for many popular patent medicines of the nineteenth century.

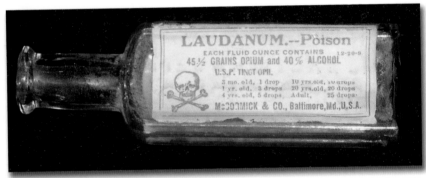

Laudanum vial, late nineteenth century

Prior to 1906, the United States had no federal legislation controlling the use of opium, or any other drug. The use of opium as a tincture, such as laudanum, had become widespread throughout the country in formulations known as *patent medicines*. These "medicines" were available in a variety of names and claimed uses, like "Mrs. Winslow's Soothing Syrup," and "paregoric."

Advertisement and label for Mrs. Winslow's Syrup

Opium and alcohol became common ingredients for treating a variety of ailments in infants, children and adults by the late nineteenth century. Many an unknowing person developed a dependence to either alcohol or opiates during this time in America. The enactment of the Federal Food and Drug Act and Administration in 1906 finally forced manufacturers to list the ingredients of their products on the label, and thus made the consumer aware of what they were ingesting. The Pure Food and Drug Act of 1906 only required contents to be labeled; it did not make any drug legal or illegal. However, there was a growing concern over the proliferation of these "patent medicines" in the country, and of course, the claims of their effectiveness and growing number of uses started to become suspect.

While the use of opium tincture, or laudanum, became popular in Europe and the United States during the time spanning the eighteenth and nineteenth century, opium use followed a different pathway into the bodies and brains of those living in China as early as 1700. The introduction of tobacco smoking in China in the seventeenth century led to the discovery of combining opium and tobacco into a pipe for smoking. Tobacco mixed with opium was called *madak,* which eventually led to the smoking of pure opium. This tradition of smoking opium for recreational use was brought to the west coast of the United States by immigrant Chinese workers in the nineteenth century.

Opium pipe

The smoking of opium involves the indirect heating of a small "globule" of opium, which at the heated temperature releases the active alkaloids, mainly morphine, as a vapor. Those who smoked opium were not aware of any of the alkaloids present in the opium sap; only that the vapors had the sought after effects of relaxation and euphoria.

The discovery of what exactly was in opium began in 1803 in Germany by a chemist named Friedrich Serturner. By dissolving opium in acid, and then neutralizing it with ammonia, he was able to isolate the alkaloid *morphine.* Morphine became the first pharmaceutical isolated from a natural product, and launched a new direction in medicine and chemistry.

Friedrich Serturner, 1803

Isolation of morphine from opium

Serturner calls this chemical "morphine," after the Greek god of dreams, Morpheus. Serturner's chemical reaction is soon replicated throughout Europe, and physicians believe that they had finally perfected the use of opium, calling morphine "God's own medicine." The discovery of the hypodermic syringe in 1843 leads to a new technique in administering morphine: directly into the vein. The effects of morphine are seen instantaneously, and much more potent than previous methods.

19th century syringe kit

The use of morphine as a potent and quick pain reliever became indispensable during the American Civil War. With the sheer number of injuries and amputations done on the battlefield, the administration of morphine made the surgeon's job easier as the patient was able to sleep and feel no pain throughout the procedure. Morphine was administered to soldiers after surgery and throughout their recovery. Their continuous need for the drug created the first wave of opiate dependent individuals, as the powerful addicting properties of morphine were unknown at the time. The addiction, or dependence, or need for morphine became known as the "soldier's disease" in post civil-war America.

During the latter half of the nineteenth century, the search began for an alternative to the powerful drugs opium and morphine, as it became increasingly clear that the pleasures and relief came with a price. The characteristics of dependence and withdrawal from these drugs were becoming obvious, and a non-addictive substitute was urgently needed.

A chemist named Felix Hoffman, working for the Bayer pharmaceutical company in Germany, set about rediscovering a chemical in 1897 that had been synthesized earlier in 1874, but had not been utilized any further at the time. The chemical was *diacetylmorphine*, the first semi-synthetic opiate. It was a product of boiling morphine and adding acetic acid in a chemical process known as acetylation. This new medicine was marketed by the Bayer company from 1898 to 1910 as a non-addictive morphine substitute and cough medicine for children. It was given the brand name Heroin, after the German word *heroisch* for heroic, which may have been used to describe how the early users of the drug felt. By 1902, Heroin sales made up 5% of the company's profits, settling in right next to aspirin on the company portfolio.

Bayer Co. ad, *New York Medical Journal*

Heroin vial from Bayer Co.

The Harrison Narcotics Tax Act of 1914 in the USA was passed to control the sale and distribution of heroin and other opiates. The law, coupled with the fact that heroin was discovered to be more addictive than morphine, led to additional legislation in 1924 banning the manufacture, sale, and use of heroin. Many other opiates were isolated and synthesized throughout the twentieth century in the search for effective painkillers that were less addictive than morphine and heroin. Codeine, a natural alkaloid of the opium plant, was isolated and used for pain relief and coughing. Oxycodone, a semi-synthetic derivative of thebaine, was introduced in 1916 and was used in

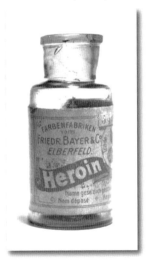

the commercial preparations of Percocet and Oxycontin. A range of semi-synthetic and synthetic opiates have been formulated and introduced during the remainder of the twentieth century, each retaining the properties of the opium plant that produce the effects that make them potential drugs of abuse.

The Controlled Substance Act of 1970 classified all drugs according to their accepted *medical use* and *potential for abuse*, and created schedules in which drugs were placed. For example, a Schedule I drug would have *no* accepted medical use and a high potential for abuse. A Schedule II drug would have an accepted medical use and a less potential for abuse, and so forth through Schedule V. The opiates are classified by the DEA and the Controlled Substance Act as schedule I, II, and III drugs. Please see Appendix 4 for a listing of the drugs under the Controlled Substance Act.

Opiates/Narcotics

The opiates, or narcotics, are classified in three different categories:

Natural
Semi-synthetic
Synthetic

Natural: The naturally occurring opiates are extracted directly from the opium poppy plant and are used as a drug in the natural form. These include:

Opium
Morphine
Codeine

Semi-synthetic: The semi-synthetic opiates are drug compounds that are chemically altered variations of the naturally occurring chemicals from the opium plant. For example, heroin is the acetylated product of morphine. The semi-synthetic opiates include:

Heroin
Oxymorphone
Oxycodone
Hydromorphone
Hydrocodone
Buprenorphine

Synthetic: The synthetic opiates are chemically created drugs that are not made from the natural opiates, but are completely synthetic and designed by chemists to have similar properties and actions of opiates, but with improved characteristics regarding pharmacokinetics, side effects, and less potential for abuse. The synthetic opiates include:

Meperidine
Fentanyl
Methadone

Effects and Actions

All of the opiates are used for the same symptoms or needed effects of the drug. This includes analgesia for moderate to severe pain, sedation, cough suppression, and diarrhea. The effects produced by the narcotics are summarized in the following table.

Short Term Effects of Opiates

ANALGESIA
SEDATION
DROWSINESS
LETHARGY
EUPHORIA
CONSTIPATION
ITCHING
TREMORS
SWEATING
INABILITY TO URINATE
RESPIRATORY DEPRESSION
CONSTRICTED PUPILS

Toxicity or overdosage of opiates involves respiratory depression and cardiac arrest.

As an opiate is taken for an extended period of time, an individual begins to develop *tolerance* for the drug. Recall from the pharmacology information that tolerance is the increased need for a drug to produce the same effects. As any of the opiates are taken over time, the user feels the need to take more of the drug to achieve the same results, which may be adequate pain relief or recreational euphoria. This occurs due to the desensitization of the *mu receptors* of the central nervous system. *Mu receptors* are located throughout the human brain, spinal cord, and gastrointestinal system, and are responsible for the effectiveness of the opiates. Naturally occurring *endorphins* activate *mu receptors* and produce the effects on the human brain that are similar to the actions produced by the opiates. As discussed in the pharmacology information, drugs exert their effect on nervous system cells through receptor sites and activation of neurotransmitter systems. The opiates are strongly attracted to the *mu receptors* in the brain that activate the areas of the brain associated with the effects mentioned earlier, namely sedation, pain relief, and euphoria. The opiates also allow naturally occurring endorphins to bind to *mu receptors* as well, increasing the stimulation of the affected brain cells. The overall effect of continued use of opiates and continued *mu receptor* activation is an alteration in the receptors and a desensitization of the activated nerve cells, causing a depletion of neurotransmitter availability. The brain cells become "used up" in a sense, and the effects that have been produced by the drug begin to become less pronounced. More drug is needed to achieve the same result, the development of *tolerance,* which is so very characteristic of opiate use. With prolonged use of opiates, a physical *dependence* develops as well, which is the continuous need for the drug to avoid symptoms of *withdrawal.* The withdrawal symptoms associated with opiate dependence are listed below.

Opiate Withdrawal Symptoms

NAUSEA	ANXIETY
VOMITING	LIGHT-HEADEDNESS
DIARRHEA	DIZZINESS
IRRITABILITY	SNEEZING
RESTLESSNESS	RUNNY NOSE
INSOMNIA	YAWNING
MUSCLE ACHES	DEPRESSION
FEVER	LOSS OF APPETITE
CHILLS	LOSS OF MOTOR COORDINATION

Opiates: Natural

The naturally occurring opiates include opium, morphine, and codeine. Opium in its crude form is still available and is smoked as it has been historically for its effects. Morphine and codeine are the alkaloids of the opium plant that are extracted and used as narcotic drugs worldwide.

Morphine

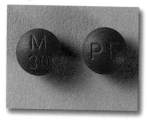

Morphine tablet

The opium plant's resin contains approximately 10 to 15% naturally occurring morphine alkaloid. As discussed earlier, it was the first alkaloid isolated from a plant in 1803, and is considered the prototypical opiate. All "opioid" medications are measured against morphine for relative potency. See Appendix 1 for a chart comparing the potencies and pharmacokinetic profiles of the opiates.

The chemical morphine is isolated from the opium plant as morphine in its active form. Let us now take a look at morphine the chemical structure:

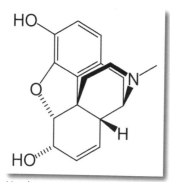

Morphine structure

Without requiring any extensive knowledge of chemistry, the information presented in this book regarding the molecular and chemical structure of the drugs of abuse will be put forward in a comparative nature, so that the subtle chemical differences among the drugs will be easily seen and hopefully understood. Notice that the chemical structure has a configuration of rings, which are comprised of carbon, nitrogen and oxygen. The –OH, or "hydroxyl groups" attached to the rings of morphine are the areas of interest to chemists, as these groups are chemically reactive and will change to form a different chemical structure under the correctly applied laboratory conditions. The basic chemical structure of the opiates will become apparent, which is a structure that is necessary for the *mu receptor* interaction and subsequent effects.

Morphine is used extensively for analgesia in hospital settings, as well as pain relief for chronic conditions of cancer, severe back pain, and other long term palliative pain control. It is used for epidural anesthesia, general anesthesia, and severe diarrhea. It is available as an IV, IM, immediate release and time release oral tablet or capsule. It is marketed under the names MS Contin®, Kadian®, Avinza®, and Oramorph® in various strengths.

Morphine is a potentially highly addictive drug, and can cause physical dependence and tolerance within a few weeks after starting use. The associated euphoria, "body high" and overall sedation of morphine is sought after by users of the drug and lend to its abuse potential. Morphine is a Schedule II drug under the Controlled Substance Act, meaning that is has an accepted medical use in this country, and a high potential for abuse.

Morphine is used illicitly by abusing injectable forms of the drug, by chewing time release oral formula tablets to defeat the extended release mechanism employed by the manufacturer, or by extracting the powder from time release capsules and snorting the powder through the nose or dissolving in water for injection. Using above the recommended dosage range is also a form of abuse, and is done frequently by those whose dependence on the drug and habitual abuse has not been for a significant amount of time.

Dosages for morphine include oral, immediate release forms of 5 to 30mg every 3 to 4 hrs. Extended release forms of 10 to 600mg every 8 to 12 hrs. IM injections are given in doses of 2.5 to 20mg every 3 to 4 hrs., and IV use includes strengths of 4 to 15mg every 4 hrs.

Street names for morphine include *M, Big M, Vitamin M, morf, Murphy, dope, all-day greys*, relating to the 100mg tablets, which are grey in color.

Street prices vary for prescription grade morphine tablets and capsules that are sold illicitly, or "on the street." Ten to twenty dollars may be able to buy any strength of tablet or capsule, immediate or extended release. Prices may average 50 cents per milligram or 1 dollar per milligram, depending on location and availability of other drugs. The extended release formulations contain a gel-like substance that may not be suitable for injecting, making the drug less desirable for many opiate abusers, and the price lower.

Codeine

In addition to morphine, the alkaloid naturally found in the opium plant in an appreciable amount is codeine, available in a quantity of approximately 1 to 3% of the opium sap. Codeine is used for mild to moderate pain relief, as well as a cough suppressant and anti-diarrheal medication. Codeine is a Schedule II drug under the Controlled Substance Act. Since codeine's pain relieving ability is not as potent as morphine or other opiates, it has been traditionally combined with other pain relievers to offer a stronger product. Codeine is commonly combined with acetaminophen, or Tylenol®, to form a product with increased pain relieving properties. The prescription drugs Tylenol #3® or Tylenol #4® are schedule III drugs under the Controlled Substance Act, designated as being less likely to be abused than morphine or codeine alone. The danger to those who do abuse these codeine combination products is the ingestion of large amounts of acetaminophen, which can become toxic to the liver. Daily ingestion of more than 4 grams of acetaminophen can become dangerous to daily liver function, and a dose of 20 grams may prove fatal.

The Tylenol® and codeine combination products contain codeine in various strengths combined with 300mg of acetaminophen per tablet. Therefore, if someone were taking 13 or more tablets daily, they would be exceeding the recommended amount of daily acetaminophen. Individuals using these products to seek the effects of stronger opiates will indeed take large quantities of acetaminophen, risking liver damage and potential liver failure. The riskiness of consuming large quantities of codeine/acetaminophen combinations is common knowledge among opiate drug abusers, and therefore these products are not abused to a great extent. The street prices of Tylenol® products with codeine are generally inexpensive, ranging from $1 per tablet to 3 tablets for $5. Codeine-only tablets are rarely prescribed and are generally not a drug that is seen being sold on the street.

Chemically, codeine can be compared with morphine, the other naturally occurring alkaloid of the opium plant.

Morphine structure

Codeine structure

The same basic ring structure is present in morphine and codeine, but the difference chemically is the—CH3, or "methyl groups," that are attached to the rings. Chemically, these methyl groups make codeine less soluble in water and less likely to be utilized as an injectable drug, but absorbed well by the body after oral administration. The codeine chemical structure has a less natural affinity for the *mu receptor*, and therefore does not produce the pain-relieving, euphoric effects of morphine. Codeine is metabolized, or broken down, to morphine by the liver, as the differentiating methyl groups are removed. The effects that are produced by codeine are mainly due to the morphine metabolite of codeine. Roughly 5 to 10% of codeine will be converted to morphine in this manner. The overall effect is that codeine produces less euphoria and analgesia than morphine, and reaches less *mu receptors* in the brain.

Opiates: Semi-synthetic
The semi-synthetic opiates include heroin, oxymorphone, oxycodone, hydromorphone, hydrocodone, and buprenorphine.

Heroin

As mentioned earlier, heroin is the acetylated product of morphine.

Heroin

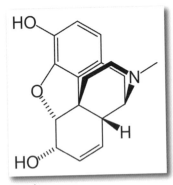

Morphine   *Heroin*

The substitution of the –OH groups on the morphine rings with the =O groups via the acetylation process produces *diacetylmorphine,* or heroin from morphine, a drug that is able to cross the blood brain barrier much more quickly. Once in the brain, heroin metabolizes quickly to morphine. Heroin in essence provides a more rapid means of getting morphine to the *mu receptors* in the brain. Heroin is less soluble in water than morphine, but more soluble in oils and fats, and must be directly injected into the bloodstream. It is not used orally, as it breaks down prior to reaching the brain. Heroin is used via intravenous injection (IV) and is termed "shooting up," "slamming," "banging," and "mainlining." It is also used by snorting through the nose, especially by novice users who do not find using a needle appealing. Heroin powder is dissolved in water, heated or "cooked" to dissolve more easily.

Cooking heroin

Heroin is also available as "tar" or "black tar," a gummier and less powder-like form of heroin. It is produced primarily in Mexico and gets its appearance and consistency from the use of a different acetylating agent in the production process. Black tar heroin and powder forms of heroin have equal potency. The consistency of black tar heroin makes it more difficult to dissolve completely for IV use, but a more effective form for smoking.

Black tar heroin

Heroin goes by the street names of *H, smack, horse, dope, black tar, tar.* It is packaged in small bags known as "stamp bags." A stamp bag of heroin may contain approximately 50mg of powder with a purity content of heroin ranging from 40% to 90%. The bags are packaged in "bundles" of 10 bags and sold as a "bundle," currently for around $100 in most U.S. cities. Fifty (50) bags is a "brick," and may be transported by dealers in this fashion.

A dose of heroin for recreational use depends on the frequency of use and the degree of tolerance within an individual. First-time users may only require 20mg, or ½ of a stamp bag, and a heavy, long-time user may need nearly 200mg, or 4 to 5 stamp bags per dose.

The onset of the effects of heroin depends on the route of administration, as do all drugs. IV use produces euphoric effects within 30 seconds, producing a "rush" of feelings for the

Bundles of heroin

user. Snorting produces effects within 3 to 5 minutes; smoking produces immediate effects, but does not provide the "rush" associated with IV use.

Heroin is classified by the Controlled Substance Act as a Schedule I drug, meaning that is has no accepted medical use in the U.S. and has a very high potential for abuse.

Oxymorphone

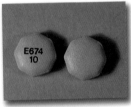

A potent opiate for the relief of moderate to severe pain, oxymorphone is sold under the brand name Opana® in the U.S. It is semi-synthetic in that it is a chemical derivative of thebaine, a minor alkaloid of the opium poppy plant.

Oxymorphone tablet

Oxymorphone

Again, the ever-present ring structure of the opiates is obvious, with the chemical difference of oxymorphone being the =O, or "double-bonded oxygen" portion of the molecule in the lower left corner. This particular formation of a chemical is called a *ketone* and leads to a more biologically active, potent drug. The *"oxy"* in the name *oxy*morphone comes from the prominent oxygens in the drug molecule. Compare with morphine:

Oxymorphone   *Morphine*

Similar, yet the specific chemical alterations discussed enable the new drug molecule to behave differently in the human body by crossing the blood-brain barrier more quickly, penetrating areas of the brain and activating *mu receptors* more efficiently, and remaining active in the nervous system for various periods of time.

Opana®, the brand name of the drug, has been utilized to a greater extent in the U.S. as an alternative to Oxycontin®; as the latter drug has gained a notorious reputation in many parts of the country. However, oxymorphone is a Schedule II drug under the Controlled Substance Act, and has a high abuse potential as well. Opana® is available as an extended-release tablet in strengths of 5mg, 10mg, 20mg and 40mg. The immediate release tablet is available in strengths of 5mg and 10mg. Dosages prescribed are individualized for each patient, and usually will start low and increase slowly, given every 12 hours.

Oxymorphone is regarded as having powerful, yet short-lived, euphoria-producing effects by those who take it recreationally. The tablets are chewed, crushed and snorted or dissolved and injected to bypass the time release mechanism built into the tablet. The drug has a broad absorption profile, ranging from minimal to appreciable depending on the individual, and its use orally leads to varying levels in the bloodstream. However, concurrent use of alcohol has been shown to increase the amount of the drug absorbed into the bloodstream.

Oxycodone

Oxycodone tablet

Oxycodone is a semi-synthetic opiate that is derived from the thebaine alkaloid, and has a similar chemical structure to codeine with the addition of an oxygen atom, hence the name "oxy" combined with "codone." The =O, or oxygen in the lower right corner of the chemical structure replaces the –OCH3 chemical group found naturally in codeine and makes the chemical a ketone. This chemical group, as well as the additional oxygen on the molecule, renders oxycodone the ability to be absorbed to a greater extent and penetrate the blood brain barrier more effectively. Furthermore, oxycodone breaks down, or metabolizes in the body to oxymorphone, an active chemical that lends to additional activity in the central nervous system.

Oxycodone

Codeine

Oxycodone was developed originally in Germany in 1916 in an effort to find a replacement for heroin and morphine. It has been marketed in the U.S. since 1939 under the familiar names of Percodan® and Percocet®, and more recently the controlled release formula Oxycontin®. Oxycodone had been available as a pain reliever in the immediate release forms of Percodan® and Percocet®, which was combined with acetaminophen for increased pain control as well as a deterrent for abuse. The extended release formula of Oxycontin® contains no acetaminophen, only oxycodone, meant to be used as a controlled release product offering pain relief over an 8 to 12 hour time period. When chewed, or crushed and snorted, or crushed and dissolved for IV injection, the controlled release mechanism within the tablet is destroyed, and the entire dosage is administered at once.

For example, an immediate release Percocet® would provide 5 mg of oxycodone per tablet, in addition to 325mg of acetaminophen, meant to provide a therapeutic effect for approximately 4 to 6 hours. A 40mg Oxycontin® tablet provides 40mg of oxycodone, meant to provide a therapeutic effect over a 12 to 24 hour period. By crushing the tablet and destroying the manufactured controlled release formulation of the product, the 40mg of oxycodone are ingested all at the same time, the equivalent of eight Percocet® tablets. Therefore, an 80mg Oxycontin® tablet will allow an individual to ingest the equivalent of 16 Percocet® tablets at a single time, without the concern of the additional acetaminophen.

Recently, the manufacturer of Oxycontin® tablets has introduced a new formulation of the tablet which embeds the medication within a glue-like matrix that makes it very difficult to extract if the pill is altered in any way. The medication will not separate from the mixture unless taken orally as intended. The new tablets are imprinted with OP instead of the OC on the older formulation.

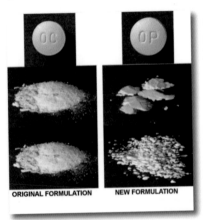

ORIGINAL FORMULATION   NEW FORMULATION

Oxycontin new formulation

Oxycodone is available in both controlled release and immediate release formulations. Roxicodone® is an immediate release brand formulation available as 5mg, 15mg, and 30mg tablets. "Roxi's" as they are referred to on the street, can vary in price from 50 cents to 1 dollar per mg.

Oxycontin, known as *OC's* or *Oxy's, 40's and 80's,* and *hillbilly heroin* are available as 10mg, 15mg, 20mg, 30mg, 40mg, 60mg, and 80mg controlled releasetablets. The 160mg version of the tablet is no longer routinely available in the U.S. As with most other illicit drugs, the street price will vary depending on the location, but generally will sell for approximately $1per mg. A prescription written by a doctor for a 30 day supply of 80mg Oxycontin®, to be taken three times a day, will place 90 tablets on the street if diverted, with a street value of $7,200 dollars. Retail value of Oxycontin® tablets are in the neighborhood of $4 a tablet, while many individuals involved in the diversion of these tablets utilize private insurance and public assistance to obtain the medication. Oxycodone is a Schedule II drug under the Controlled Substance Act, and is considered to have a very high abuse potential.

Hydromorphone

Hydromorphone is a potent, semi-synthetic opiate prescribed for analgesia and chronic pain relief, as well as cough suppression. It was developed shortly after heroin was removed from the market for its use as a potent cough relief drug. First synthesized in Germany in 1924, it was marketed under the brand name Dilaudid®, which borrowed its name from *laudanum* at the time, a potent preparation of

Hydromorphone tablet

morphine. The similarity of hydromorphone to morphine can be illustrated by comparing the chemical structure of the two drugs:

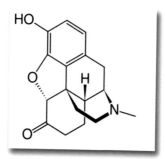

Hydromorphone

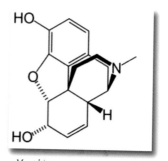

Morphine

The oxygen (O) in the lower right corner of the chemical structure does not have a hydrogen (H) attached to it, as does the morphine structure. As with the previously discussed semi-synthetic opiate chemicals, this =O structure is now a *ketone,* which is more chemically active in the human body than the naturally occurring opiate morphine. This is similar to the chemical conversion of codeine to oxydocone, resulting in a more potent drug product. The semi-synthetic nature of hydromorphone makes the drug more lipid, or fat, soluble and allows it to enter the brain more quickly. This gives hydromorphone a faster onset of action and also a higher potency than that of morphine. It is approximately eight times stronger than morphine.

The high solubility of hydromorphone makes it a good drug for oral use in addition to IV injection. The oral availability of the drug lends to its use as a cough suppressant, offering effective blood levels after 30 to 60 minutes. It also tends to cause less nausea than morphine in users, as well as less histamine release effects such as itching. Hydromorphone is available in the U.S. in an immediate release formulation only at this time. Other countries of the world use the sustained release versions of the drug for chronic pain relief. The sustained release formulation of the drug is also being used in opiate addiction treatment programs as a substitute for methadone, as the shorter half life of the drug and less bothersome side effect profile make hydromorphone a better choice for patients.

The most common brand name of hydromorphone used in the U.S. is Dilaudid®, however, many generic products are on the market. It is available in immediate release tablets of 0.5mg, 1mg, 2mg, 3mg, 4mg and 8mg; cough syrup of 1mg/5ml; 3mg suppository, and injectables of 1mg/ml, 2mg/ml, 4mg/ml and 8mg/ml. Hydromorphone is sold on the street under the names *drugstore heroin, hospital heroin, k1, k2, k4, k8* (derived from the misinterpretation of the Abbot symbol and number imprinted on the tablet, (see start of this section)), *D, dillies, moose,* and others.

The tablets are the most commonly seen form of the drug on the street, and sell for approximately $1per mg (8mg tablets selling for $10 each). The drug may be taken orally, crushed and snorted, or dissolved and injected IV. Hydromorphone is a Schedule II drug under the Controlled Substance Act.

Hydrocodone

Hydrocodone tablet

Hydrocodone is a powerful, semi-synthetic opiate most commonly used as an agent for moderate pain relief and as a cough suppressant. It retains its chemical properties when taken orally, and thus does not break down significantly when taken by mouth. Therefore, it is available in tablet, capsule, and syrup form. Hydrocodone is marketed under various brand names, such as Vicodin®, Lortab®, Hycodan®, Norco® and Tussionex®, as well as numerous generic versions. Hydrocodone has been in use in the U.S. since the FDA approved it in 1943 under the brand name Hycodan®. Hydrocodone is a semi-synthetic, chemical derivative of codeine. Compare the two drugs' chemical structures:

Hydrocodone

Codeine

The –Me groups refer to methyl (CH3) groups. The two chemicals are very similar, with the difference being in the lower portion of the chemical and the loss of hydrogen (H) atoms. This chemical alteration makes hydrocodone a ketone structure with increased chemical activity in the human body. Hydrocodone also "breaks down," or metabolizes in the body to another active opiate, hydromorphone. It is the active metabolite of hydromorphone that accounts for a large part of the potency and activity of hydrocodone.

Hydrocodone is most commonly formulated as a combination drug, adding acetaminophen as an additional pain-relieving drug in most preparations. The most commonly prescribed brand name drugs, such as Vicodin® and Lortab®, combine strengths of 5mg to 10mg of hydrocodone with 500mg to 750mg of acetaminophen in each tablet. It is not uncommon for a hydrocodone abuser to ingest 10,000 to 20,000mg of acetaminophen in a single day. It is this large amount of acetaminophen per tablet that makes these combination products a dangerous drug of abuse, as the large doses of acetaminophen that may be consumed in a day may prove to be damaging to the liver and even fatal to the user. Seasoned drug users are aware of this drawback of the hydrocodone combination products, making these products less than the "drug of choice" of opiate users. However, hydrocodone use continues to escalate in the U.S. and now constitutes one of the most abused substances in the country. The combination products of hydrocodone and acetaminophen, available in generic form, are classified under the Controlled Substance Act as a Schedule III drug. These products contain less than 15mg of hydrocodone per unit. Restrictions are fewer which allows for increased prescribing ability by doctors and less stringent control by providers, as well as the perception of hydrocodone being a less abusable substance. For example, DEA and state regulations prohibit "phone-in" or prescriptions telephoned by a doctor to a pharmacy for Schedule II medications. However, for Schedule III drugs, this is permitted. Inventory controls for pharmacies are less intensive, with estimation being a common practice rather than actual counting with Schedule II drugs. This allows for opportunity for diversion from pharmacy stock, and "bogus" call-in or forged prescriptions.

The selling price of *vikes* or *tabs, 357's* or *hydros* can be from $2 to $10 per tablet depending on the strength and geographical area. Cough syrups containing hydrocodone, such as Hycodan®, Histussin HC®, PV Tussin®, and a variety of generic manufacturer names, can be found for $20 to $40 per 8 oz. bottle. These products contain antihistamines, expectorants and decongestants as well as hydrocodone. The syrup usually contains 5mg of hydrocodone per teaspoonful.

Summary of semi-synthetic opiates

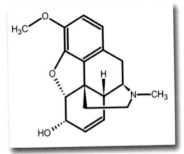

Morphine

Oxymorphone

Hydromorphone

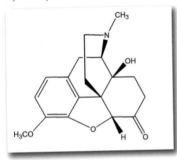

Oxycodone

Codeine

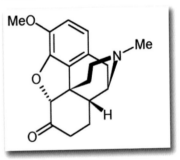

Hydrocodone

Buprenorphine

Buprenorphine tablet

Buprenorphine is a semi-synthetic opiate, which also has the distinction of being a *partial agonist* and *antagonist,* meaning that the drug will have an opiate-like effect on *mu receptors,* but also has an antagonistic or blocking effect as well. This dual effect is unique to buprenorphine and has led to its use as

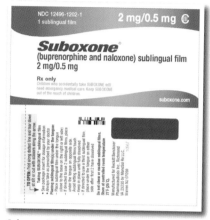

Suboxone Film

an analgesic as well as a medicine to treat an opiate dependence. The analgesic has been marketed as Buprenex® in the parenteral (IV) form, and Suboxone® and Subutex® for use in opiate addiction treatment. Suboxone® and Subutex® are available as sublingual tablets that are dissolved in the mouth, under the tongue. The drug is metabolized considerably when used orally, and does not reach appropriate and effective bloodstream levels. Suboxone and Subutex have recently been made available as a sublingual film, which is dissolved under the tongue in a similar manner as the tablet. The film supposedly dissolves faster than the tablet, and is less bitter tasting. The individual packaging is more convenient, difficult to open to prevent accidental ingestion, and contains an imprinted code for tracking purposes.

The chemical structure of buprenorphine:

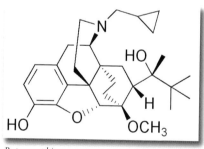

Buprenorphine

Buprenorphine is a derivative of thebaine, an alkaloid of the opium plant. The *partial agonist* quality of buprenorphine means that when it binds to a receptor, it is less likely to cause a response that a full agonist such as morphine or codeine. It also has a high affinity, or bonding ability, to the receptors, and prevents other opiates from exerting their effects. This less than full effect on the opiate receptors, coupled with its chemical bonding capability makes buprenorphine useful in preventing the use of other opiates, thus a powerful tool in treating an opiate addicted individual. Buprenorphine has a long elimination half life due to its high affinity for receptors, which is in the range of 20-73 hours, being highly dependent on individual variables.

The use of buprenorphine for opiate dependence treatment became possible in the U.S. with the passage of the Drug Addiction Treatment Act of 2000, that made it possible for doctors to treat opiate addiction by prescribing opiates themselves, a practice that had been illegal for most of the twentieth century.

Buprenorphine is available as Subutex® which contains buprenorphine in the strengths 2mg and 8mg. It is also available as Suboxone®, which contains 2mg and 8mg buprenorphine in combination with the opiate antagonist drug naloxone in a 4:1 ratio (buprenorphine 8mg : naloxone 2mg). The inclusion of naloxone in the drug preparation is to discourage the IV use of the drug, as the naloxone will provide additional opiate blockade at the receptor sites if injected, but is not effective when used as intended, sublingually. The maximum daily dose of buprenorphine is 32mg, which is also a "ceiling dose," as the drug exerts no additional effects above this dosage.

Due to its perceived safety profile and less potential for causing an overdose, buprenorphine is classified as a Schedule III drug under the Controlled Substance Act. It can therefore be prescribed via telephone by a physician and refilled at a pharmacy. This designation has made buprenorphine a much more convenient medication to use in the treatment of opiate dependence.

Buprenorphine has developed into a recreational drug regardless, and is typically sought and used by opiate users when the drug of choice is unavailable, or when one wishes to attempt to stop using opiates on their own. The partial agonist nature of the drug gives it a long onset of action time frame, which is close to 2 hours, and a long time to peak effects if taken sublingually as directed. These characteristics make buprenorphine an unlikely drug of choice for an opiate user looking for a "high." Buprenorphine will produce effects of analgesia and a sense of euphoria in an individual with low opiate tolerance. Crushing and sniffing, in addition to injecting, is also practiced by those with a higher tolerance. The increased use of buprenorphine for opiate addiction treatment has led to an illicit market in the U.S. *Bupes, subbies, oranges, stop signs,* or *subs* sell for $10 to $15 per 8mg tablet on the street.

Opiates: Synthetic

The synthetic opiates include fentanyl, meperidine, and methadone.

Fentanyl

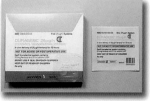

Fentanyl is an entirely synthetic opiate, synthesized in 1959 by Janssen Pharmaceutica laboratories. It was developed for use as an analgesic and an anesthetic, and was originally marketed as Sublimaze®, an intravenous anesthetic. The chemical structure of fentanyl is:

Fentanyl patch

Fentanyl is the most powerful opiate known, with a potency of approximately 80 times that of morphine. The chemical structure of fentanyl bears little resemblance to the ringed structure of morphine and the semi-synthetic chemicals that are based on the structure of morphine. The synthetic nature of the fentanyl chemical lends to the drugs potency, as well as its rapid and short

Fentanyl

acting activity. It was marketed as alfentanil and sufentanil, potent and short acting analgesics for use in surgery.

The Janssen Pharmaceutica company also developed fentanyl in a patch form in the mid 1990's, for use in chronic pain patients, as fentanyl continued to be recognized as the best opiate pain reliever available for chronic pain patients, especially cancer pain. The idea of the transdermal patch is to wear a patch on the skin and allow the powerful drug to slowly be absorbed over a long period of time. This would allow for a potent pain reliever to be at therapeutic blood levels consistently and allow for continuous pain relief.

The fentanyl patch was sold as Duragesic®, and provides active drug for 48 to 72 hours while worn on the skin. The drug is placed in an alcohol-based gel within a reservoir between two layers, one layer which acts as a backing, or outer layer, and another layer which allows the drug to diffuse through to the patient's skin. Fentanyl is fat soluble, thus the drug is absorbed through the skin into fat deposits, and slowly released into the body.

Duragesic® brand patches and fentanyl generic patches are available in five different patch sizes: 12.5 micrograms (mcg) per hour, 25mcg/hr, 50mcg/hr, 75mcg/hr, and 100mcg/hr. The rate of diffusion of the drug through the patch's membrane is fairly constant, thus the strength of the patch is determined by its size, with a larger patch containing more drug and releasing more per hour. Initially placed on the skin, the drug will take effect within 8 to 12 hours, and remain relatively constant for 48 to 72 hours.

Fentanyl shares the side effect profile associated with the other opiate drugs, most notably respiratory depression and central nervous system depression. Malfunction of patches causing excessive release of drug, as well as the unpredictable nature of fat-soluble drugs such as fentanyl have led to the drug causing overdoses and severe side effects. Fentanyl has a high bioavailability when absorbed through the skin (over 90%), less when used buccally (50%), and even lower with the oral route (33%). However, when the integrity of the patch system is broken, and the drug is retrieved directly, the time release mechanism of the patch is broken and the drug is placed in the system directly. This is the common method of illicitly using fentanyl.

The transdermal patch is cut into pieces, allowing the drug to seep out of the cut edge. The "piece" of patch is then placed between the cheek and gum and sucked on to obtain the drug through the buccal route. Although the drug does not reach the intended fat deposits in this manner and the availability is reduced, the drug is allowed to enter the system freely without the time-release membrane of the patch control. The buccal route also allows for increased access to blood circulation and transport of drug into the central nervous system. Habitual users of fentanyl describe its effects as similar to those of heroin, with increased sedation and not as long lasting.

Because the effects of fentanyl are strong, yet last for only a short time, users of the drug can become dependent and addicted very quickly. The potency of fentanyl can lead to unsuspecting overdoses, even in those individuals with an acquired opiate tolerance. Fentanyl is usually sold illicitly in the patch form, for prices ranging from $20 to $30 for a single 50 "mic" patch, and $40 to $50 for a 100mcg patch. Used patches that have been discarded after use may still contain a significant amount of the drug, and drug abusers have been known to search for used patches in trash containers of hospitals, health-care centers, and patient homes.

Fentanyl is a Schedule II drug under the Controlled Substance Act. The transdermal patch is the most commonly prescribed as well as diverted and abused formulation of the drug. In addition to sucking the gel out of the patch, it can also be smoked, snorted or injected. Fentanyl powder is also used by drug dealers as an additive or substitute for heroin, creating a dangerously potent mixture that is often mistakenly misused and overdosed. *Magic* and *the bomb* are a few of the names on the street for the fentanyl and heroin mixture. *"China White"* refers to chemical analogs of illicit Fentanyl produced in clandestine labs.

Meperidine

Meperidine was synthesized in 1939, not as an opiate, but as an antimuscarinic, or anticholinergic drug to treat muscle spasms. Its analgesic properties were discovered by accident as it provided relief for acute, moderate to severe pain in

Meperidine tablet

patients suffering from various forms of muscle spasm. Meperidine, or Demerol®, the trade name of the drug, became the opioid of choice for many physicians throughout the 20th century as it was perceived as being safer than morphine and less addicting. It is a more lipid (fat) soluble chemical than morphine, and is structurally more similar to atropine and other antispasmodics than to morphine.

Meperidine   *Morphine*

The high lipid solubility of the drug allows for a faster onset of action, with effects being felt within 10 to 15 minutes, making the drug an excellent choice for fast relief of acute pain. The duration of action is usually between 2 and 3 hours. Meperidine is metabolized quickly by the liver, with the accumulation of metabolites that have neurotoxic properties, a unique characteristic of meperidine. The metabolic properties of meperidine and the buildup of toxic byproducts make the drug possibly interact with other medications, including benzodiazepines, antidepressants and alcohol. Meperidine's chemical similarity to the antispasmodics lends to an increased interaction and side effect profile, including aggravating convulsion disorders and cardiac abnormalities.

The fast onset of action of the drug has made it susceptible to abuse, with a "rush" and increased euphoria associated with its use. Tolerance to the drug develops very quickly, as the duration of the drug is not very extensive, and more is needed in a short period of time.

Meperidine is a Schedule II drug under the Controlled Substance Act. It is available as 50mg and 100mg tablets, a 50mg per teaspoonful syrup, and injectable solutions of 25mg, 50mg, 75mg and 100mg per ml. The main route of use is either orally or by injection, with therapeutic doses for pain relief being between 50mg and 150mg every 3 to 4 hours. Most street meperidine is available as oral tablets.

Generic manufacturers of meperidine are the most commonly dispensed form of the drug, with the trade name Demerol® not used much since losing patent protection. Street names continue to refer the drug as *demmies*, referring to Demerol. Street prices for the tablets range from $8 to $15 for a 50mg tablet. Two to three tablets (100mg to 150mg) is an average dose for those individuals using meperidine illicitly and looking for a "rush." The injectable solution has been called *dummy oil* on the street, referring to its lack of potency in comparison to heroin.

Methadone

Methadone is a synthetic opiate, developed in Germany in 1937 as a possible alternative to morphine-based medication. The structure of methadone has no relationship to morphine or any other opioid drug.

Methadone liquid

Although its chemical structure is unlike morphine, methadone attaches to *mu* opiate receptors very well, leading the medical community of the 1930's to believe that it would make a good pain reliever. However, it was found to be too toxic and addictive during its initial use in Nazi Germany.

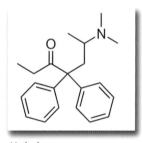

After the war, the patent for methadone was lost by German manufacturers, and the Lilly Company in the U.S. marketed the drug as an analgesic with the trade name "Dolophine." Prior to being used in the U.S., the drug was known as polamidon or "Amidon."

Methadone

Methadone did not become extensively useful as an analgesic, but developed an "on the street" reputation as being very useful in treating narcotic addiction. After clinical trials in New York City in the 1960's that utilized methadone treatment to address the growing heroin problem in that city, the drug was recognized as being able to stop illicit opiate use and relieve an individual from the physical withdrawal symptoms associated with cessation of opiate use.

Methadone is considered a full *mu-opioid agonist,* in that it binds to the opiate receptors throughout the body and has the same effect profile as an opiate. The pharmacological difference of methadone is that it has a very slow rate of metabolism and a very high rate of lipid (fat) solubility. Thus, the half-life of methadone is in the range of 15 to 60 hours (Remember that the half-life of morphine is only 2 to 3 hours). The pharmacokinetics of methadone varies greatly between individuals, and the half-life may be as much as 190 hours in some individuals. The metabolic pathways that act on methadone differ among individuals, and will result in different rates of metabolism and elimination of the drug. This long half-life allows for once-daily dosing of the drug, a convenience for treating those using the medication in outpatient methadone clinics. This long half-life also contributes to the extended withdrawal symptom profile of methadone, making quitting the drug difficult. Nausea and vomiting, insomnia, muscle aches and irritability may all continue for weeks.

Methadone has a high rate of bioavailability when taken orally, again making the drug easy to use in the clinic setting. It has no further advantages when injected, producing no "rush" of effects. Methadone goes into other body tissues and reaches its peak effect at about the same rate whether taken orally or by IV injection. Methadone is available as an oral solution, oral diskette for dissolving into solution, and oral tablets.

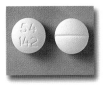
Methadone tablet

Methadone is mainly used in the treatment of opiate addiction, acting as substitute therapy to allow for intervention and psychosocial improvement for a patient. It has also been used in pain management programs, treating chronic pain that does not respond to other medications. Methadone provides good bioavailability, as well as being a long acting agent useful in combination with a fast acting drug.

Methadone diversion has become an increasing problem, with more methadone being used by physicians for pain, and methadone clinics treating more patients for opiate dependence. Methadone is sought out on the street not as a drug of choice, but as an alternative to withdrawal from one's drug of choice. Methadone also has a synergistic response when taken with alcohol or benzodiazepines, causing one to experience increased sedation and some degree of euphoria. Although taking opiates with methadone will produce no additional effect, as the methadone will essentially "block" the opiate from the *mu receptors,* other drugs continue to exert an effect by other neuron pathways that are increased by methadone. These interactions are well known among users of methadone, and the use of multiple drugs, or "polypharmacy" is common.

The street price of methadone can be as high as $1 per 1mg. Names on the street includes *meth, dose, and juice.* Average doses for patients receiving methadone in a clinic setting can be between 80mg to 100mg once a day, with lower doses used by physicians for chronic pain treatment, usually in the 40mg to 60mg per day in divided doses. Most clinics will utilize methadone oral solution, while those prescribed for pain will receive methadone tablets, 5mg or 10mg.

Miscellaneous Opiates

Propoxyphene

A weak opioid agonist, propoxyphene is a synthetic analgesic prepared in combination with acetaminophen and marketed under the brand name Darvocet-N®. It is prescribed for mild to moderate pain relief. Propoxyphene has abuse potential and is a schedule IV drug under the Controlled Substance Act. The drug is usually sought when a drug of choice is unavailable and an opiate is needed in the short term. The tablets of propoxyphene are either taken orally, crushed and snorted, or mixed into an aqueous solution and injected. Withdrawal symptoms have been reported to occur when propoxyphene use stops, with effects similar to other opiate withdrawal symptoms. Propoxyphene tablets contain 100mg of propoxyphene and 650mg of acetaminophen. Street prices may be $2 per tablet, depending on area and supply. Propoxyphene was removed from the US market by the FDA in November of 2010, as the drug had been associated with heart abnormalities.

Tramadol

Tramadol is a centrally acting opiate agonist that is prescribed for moderate to severe pain. A synthetic drug chemically related to codeine, it is marketed under the brand name Ultram® in tablets of 50mg strength. It is also formulated in a combination tablet, Ultracet® with acetaminophen in strengths of 37.5mg and 325mg of acetaminophen. It is also available in a generic form as an extended release (ER) tablet in strengths of 100mg, 200mg, and 300mg.

When taken at higher than therapeutic doses, tramadol has the potential to produce effects of euphoria in the user, as well as improvements in feelings of depression and anxiety. The mechanism of action of tramadol includes not only opiate mu receptor activity but serotonin and norepinephrine activity as well, which may account for the effects of improved anxiety. Tramadol also produces dependence and withdrawal symptoms similar to those of the opiates. Currently, tramadol is not a controlled substance in the U.S., but several states have placed the drug under a Schedule IV designation. Known on the street as *Ultras* or *trammies*, the tablets are taken orally in doses exceeding 300mg, can be crushed and snorted, or injected IV. Street value is around $2 per tablet.

Stimulants

Stimulants are the class of drugs that include cocaine, amphetamines, and related compounds generally referred to as "uppers." Nicotine and caffeine are also stimulants, widely used but less potent than the stronger, more abused drugs such as cocaine and methamphetamine. These chemicals are characterized by their ability to increase alertness, decrease the need for sleep, heighten arousal, and produce euphoria in the user. Energized feelings accompany the ability to perform tasks for extended periods of time. All of the stimulants affect the neurotransmitter systems of dopamine, norepinephrine and serotonin in ways that result in increased energy and activation of the reward centers of the brain. It is this activity that makes the stimulants highly abused. By increasing the availability of the neurotransmitters dopamine, norepinephrine and serotonin, stimulants produce a rapid or irregular heartbeat, increase in blood pressure, increase in metabolism and energy, and arousal of the brain's reward center, resulting in a condition that leads to craving more of the drug. Tolerance to stimulant use quickly develops and increasing dosages are needed to produce effects. Withdrawal from stimulants may lead to fatigue and depression, insomnia and irritability.

Effects and Actions

Short Term Effects of Stimulants

INCREASED ENERGY
DECREASED APPETITE
MENTAL ALERTNESS
INCREASED HEART RATE AND BLOOD PRESSURE
INCREASED TEMPERATURE
DILATED PUPILS

Adverse Effects of Stimulants

TREMORS
RESTLESSNESS/INSOMNIA
BLURRED VISION
BUZZING IN EARS
SEVERE HEADACHE
NAUSEA/VOMITING
GRINDING OF TEETH

Long Term Effects of Stimulants

CHEST PAINS
IRREGULAR HEARTBEAT
HEART ATTACK
LUNG DAMAGE
PANIC ATTACKS
DEPRESSION
DELUSIONS AND HALLUCINATIONS
"COCAINE BUGS" (SKIN SENSATION)

Stimulants may be of a *natural source,* which include cocaine, caffeine, nicotine, and khat. The *synthetic* stimulants include amphetamines, methylphenidate, and the anorectics, which are used as appetite suppressants, or "diet pills." The drugs of abuse will exclude caffeine and nicotine in this discussion.

Cocaine

Brick of processed cocaine

Coca plant (Erythroxylon coca)

"Woe to you, my Princess, when I come... you shall see who is the stronger, a gentle little girl who doesn't eat enough or a big wild man who has cocaine in his body."
-Sigmund Freud

"There's no happy ending to cocaine. You either die, you go to jail, or else you run out."
-Sam Kinison

History
Cocaine originates as an alkaloid found in the leaves of the shrub *Erythroxylon coca,* found in the Andes Mountains of Columbia, Peru and Bolivia. The leaves of the plant have been chewed by inhabitants of these areas for the past 5000 years. The coca from the chewed leaves provided stimulating and hunger-reducing effects to the indigenous people living in the high altitudes of the mountains.

During the Spanish conquest of South America in the 16th century, the practice of coca leaf chewing and the perceived effects were discovered by the Europeans, who became curious about the use of the plant. Leaves of the plant were occasionally brought back to Europe, but suffered degradation during the long trip and did not provide the same effect. As the knowledge of chemistry began to improve during the 19th century, the coca leaves were subjected to many processes by various German scientists, with the isolation of the alkaloid "erythroxyline" in 1855. A scientist by the name of Albert Niemann earned his Ph.D. for his publication describing the purification process of "cocaine," named after the coca plant with the common "-ine" suffix given to alkaloids.

During the latter half of the 19th century, the powdered, isolated form of cocaine became very popular in Europe, as it was considered beneficial by many members of the medical community. "Invigorating and Exhilarating" were some of the words used to describe the effects of cocaine, as it was prescribed for depression and digestive disorders, as well as alcoholism and morphine addiction, and a variety of other ailments. Sigmund Freud used cocaine frequently and wrote of his experiences in a monograph titled "Uber Coca." He utilized cocaine in the treatment of his patients also, and maintained a position that the drug was non-addictive.

The general population of Europe began to appreciate the effects of cocaine as well, as products such as "Vin Mariani" became extremely popular. The concoction combined wine and cocaine, as ethanol will extract the cocaine alkaloid from the leaves very readily.

**POPULAR
FRENCH TONIC WINE**
Fortifies and Refreshes Body + Brain
Restores Health and Vitality

Cocaine products began to reach the United States in the late 19th century in the form of cigars, cigarettes, inhalants, medicinal drinks and drops, injectables, as well as the popular "Vin Mariani."

An interesting use of the drug was popularized by Mr. John Pemberton, a pharmacist from Georgia. Due to the growing public concern with alcohol use, Mr. Pemberton added a "pinch of coca leaves" and caffeine to soda water and named his drink "Coca-Cola." It was an instant success, and launched an American empire. (Coca leaves were removed from the product in 1906.)

By the early twentieth century widespread cocaine abuse began to appear throughout the United States, and the 1914 Harrison Narcotics Act included cocaine as a prohibited "narcotic." The patented products which contained cocaine became unavailable, and the use of cocaine became an underground activity. What was once considered a beneficial medicine and popular recreational drug was now prohibited, restricted, and generally considered the "third scourge of the human race" after alcohol and opium.

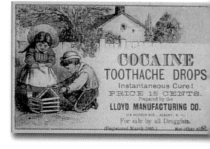

**COCAINE
TOOTHACHE DROPS**
Instantaneous Cure!
PRICE 15 CENTS.
Prepared by the
LLOYD MANUFACTURING CO.
219 HUDSON AVE., ALBANY, N. Y.
For sale by all Druggists.

Further refinement processes throughout the 20th century produced cocaine powder, which became popular in the 1970's. This form of the drug is insufflated, or "snorted" through the nose, as well as injected IV. The 1980's saw the rise of freebase or "crack" cocaine which is smoked.

Cocaine Production

The leaves of the coca plant contain on average 0.8% cocaine as an alkaloid. The concentration is dependent on the freshness of the leaves and the environment in which the plant has grown. The cooler, higher altitudes produce a harvest of a generally higher concentration plant. The leaves of the plant are stripped from the bush by hand and sun dried for 1 to 2 days. If not dried immediately, or exposed to moisture and humidity, the leaves will rot quickly, decompose, and lose potency. The cocaine alkaloid will remain stable in the dried leaf, which is suitable for packing and travel.

Forms and Use

There are three *forms* of cocaine which are products of the process: coca paste, coke base, and cocaine hydrochloride.

Coca paste

Coca leaves are macerated (mashed), mixed with lime, water and kerosene in a barrel or pit, and mixed vigorously for several hours. The lime acts as a base and extracts the cocaine alkaloid from the leaf, and the kerosene as a solvent. After filtering the solvent, sulfuric acid is added to the mixture to convert the cocaine base form to cocaine sulfate, which is water soluble. Lime is added again, which converts cocaine sulfate back to its base form, which precipitates out of the solution as a gummy solid, which is coca paste. The coca paste now contains cocaine in the amount of 30% to 80%.

Coke base

Coke base is a product derived from purifying the coca paste. The coca paste is dissolved again with dilute sulfuric acid and concentrated potassium permanganate, until the solution is colorless. Dilute ammonia is added to neutralize the cocaine sulfate to produce a solid precipitate, purified coke base. Once dried, the coke base can be packaged for travel to a laboratory for the production of cocaine hydrochloride.

Cocaine hydrochloride

Cocaine hydrochloride is typically produced in small batches of 1kg to 5kg in size. Coke base is dissolved with diethyl ether, acetone, and hydrochloric acid to produce a precipitate of white, flaky crystals, cocaine hydrochloride. The crystallization process takes from 3 to 6 hours, after which the product is heat dried, pressed and packaged. The crystalline powder cocaine hydrochloride contains between 80 to 97% cocaine, and appears as an off-white or white powder.

Forms of Cocaine

Crack cocaine

Powder cocaine

Cocaine is predominantly available in two forms: The base or "freebase" form of the drug, and the salt form of cocaine hydrochloride (cocaine HCl). Cocaine HCl is very soluble in water and can be snorted or injected, while the base form is not soluble in water. However, cocaine base vaporizes at a lower temperature and is suitable for smoking, whereas cocaine HCl will burn and not vaporize. Smoking freebase cocaine, or which is more commonly known as "crack" cocaine, has become a very popular method of ingesting cocaine. By dissolving powder cocaine in water and adding sodium bicarbonate (baking soda), a "rock" form will precipitate out of solution containing a cocaine/bicarbonate/water mixture. Upon burning of the "rock," the water will boil and make a "cracking" sound.

Pharmacology

Cocaine exists as a natural alkaloid, with a unique 2-ring chemical structure:

As mentioned earlier, cocaine affects the neurotransmitter *dopamine* in the central nervous system. In short, cocaine binds to a protein identified as the dopamine

Cocaine

transporter, and blocks the function of the transporter protein, which is to remove excess dopamine from the nerve cell synapse. This creates an excess of dopamine and the "rush" effects of the drug.

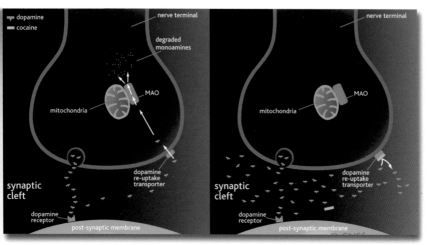

The pharmacokinetics of cocaine is dependent on the form of the drug and the route of use. When smoked, crack cocaine produces results in less than 10 seconds, and may last 5 to 10 minutes. IV administration of the drug produces similar results to smoking. Insufflation, or snorting cocaine powder, will produce effects in about 15 minutes and may last up to one hour.

Regardless of the route of administration, cocaine is a drug that is rapidly eliminated from the body, with a half-life between 0.5 and 1.5 hours. Thus, continuous administration is necessary to retain a "high" feeling. Breakdown products of cocaine remain in the body, and can be detected in the urine for several days after use.

The following table summarizes the different routes of cocaine administration and the various pharmacological differences:

Route	Form	Onset	Peak	Duration
Insufflation (Snorting)	Cocaine HCl (powder)	3 to 5 minutes	30 to 60 minutes	1 to 2 hours
Smoking	Cocaine base (crack)	Immediate	1 to 3 minutes	5 to 15 minutes
Intravenous	Cocaine HCl (dissolved powder)	Immediate	1 to 3 minutes	5 to 15 minutes

Cocaine powder is dosed in "lines" of approximately 4 to 6 inches long, containing typically 100mg. The lines are "snorted" through the nose by means of a straw or rolled-up paper bill. Absorption through the nasal mucosa is approximately 30-

60%. Street price of cocaine powder in the U.S. currently averages $100-$140 per gram, and $1200 to $2,000 per ounce. Purity varies, as the powder is often "cut" or diluted with ingredients such as lactose, inositol, mannitol, lidocaine, sugar, cornstarch, caffeine and various other fillers to increase the volume and profit. Cocaine is called by many names, which include *coke, snow, blow, soft, candy, and toot.*

Lines of coke

Cocaine freebase, or "crack," is dosed as "rocks" which typically weigh approximately ¼ gram and are sold in the $20 - $40 range in the U.S., depending on purity and place of sale. Dealers will also sell crack in different quantities, such as a "teener" (1/16 oz, or 1.5gm) or an "eight ball" (1/8 oz, or 3 gm), with prices varying depending on quality and location. The rocks of crack cocaine are placed in a specially prepared pipe, usually glass, which includes a bed of heavy copper or stainless steel, commonly referred to as "chore," named after *Chore Boy* brand scouring pads. The chore serves as a base on which the crack is melted and the vapors pass through into the pipe. Crack is also called *rocks, hard, nuggets, piece, and raw.*

Cocaine is also used via the intravenous route, with drug injection providing the highest blood levels in the shortest amount of time. The powder form is dissolved in water, heated and drawn into a syringe for injection. Cocaine may also be mixed with heroin for injection, producing a mixture known as a *"speedball."* Cocaine is also mixed with marijuana and smoked, which would

Crack pipe

require the base or "crack" form of the drug, as the powder will not burn properly.

Cocaine and alcohol mixed together produce a byproduct in the body known as *cocaethylene.* This chemical has a long duration of action, particularly in the brain, and may have toxic effects. This combination of cocaine and alcohol use has resulted in a large number of reported drug-related deaths.

Cocaine is a Schedule II drug under the Controlled Substance Act, as it does have a medical purpose as a local anesthetic, used in certain surgical procedures involving the eye and nasal ducts. The –ine is used in medical literature to name anesthetics ("coca" + -"ine"). The "numb" feeling experienced by cocaine users when snorting the powder or applying directly to the gums is due to the drug's anesthetic properties. The long term effects of cocaine use include depression, heart irregularities, respiratory failure, strokes, irritation of the nasal septum, and gastrointestinal complications.

"Annual U.S. revenue for Starbucks®, 2005 = $6.4 billion"
"Annual U.S. revenue for cocaine, 2005 = $70 billion"

Amphetamines

The group of drugs known as *amphetamines* has been used historically to produce increased wakefulness and focus, and decreased fatigue and appetite. Thus, these drugs have been prescribed to treat attention deficit hyperactivity disorder (ADHD), narcolepsy, and as an aid in appetite suppression and diet. The drugs prescribed include dextroamphetamine, brand names Dexedrine® and Dextrostat®; the mixed chemical salts of dextroamphetamine and amphetamine, brand name Adderall®; lisdexamfetamine, brand name Vyvanse®; and methamphetamine, brand name Desoxyn®.

History

Amphetamine was first synthesized in Germany in 1887, and identified as a chemical similar to ephedrine, which had been isolated from the natural chemical *ephedra,* or *ma-huang* in China, from the *Ephedra sinica* plant. Ma-huang had been used for centuries by physicians in China as an herbal remedy.

Ephedrine

Amphetamine

The synthetic amphetamine was found to be structurally similar to ephedrine, and produced similar feelings of reduced appetite and heightened energy. Ephedrine was also being used for its bronchodilating properties in the treatment of asthma.

As ephedrine was derived from the naturally occurring ephedra, a synthetic substitute was needed by the 1920's as fear of supply shortages became a concern. Amphetamine was recruited as that substitute, and was first marketed in 1932 as the Benzedrine® inhaler, which contained 250mg of amphetamine in a cotton plug for nasal inhalation.

As the inhalers gained popularity in the U.S., the amphetamine inside was abused as the container was opened and the drug removed for oral and/or IV use.

The first oral tablet form of amphetamine was introduced to the world in 1937 by the Smith, Kline and French company under the trade name Dexedrine®. This form of the drug was the dextro-amphetamine form, referring to the particular configuration of the chemical (dextro=right, levo=left). Dexedrine® was prescribed for narcolepsy, attention disorders, depression and obesity.

World War II saw extensive use of amphetamines for its ability to increase alertness and decrease fatigue. Casual and recreational use of amphetamines flourished throughout the 1950's and 1960's in the U.S., as the prescription stimulant was perceived as not being dangerous, and also as a replacement for the now illegal cocaine. Under the Controlled Substance Act of 1970, dextroamphetamine and other amphetamines are designated Schedule II, as they have a high potential for abuse for a drug with approved medical uses.

The word amphetamine is derived from the chemical name alpha-methylphenethylamine.

Pharmacology

Similar to cocaine, amphetamines exert their effects through the neurotransmitters dopamine, serotonin, and norepinephrine in the brain. The areas of the brain affected by dopamine are particularly affected by amphetamine. As it was discussed regarding cocaine's ability to block the reuptake of dopamine, and thus increase the amount of dopamine available to the brain, so is the case with amphetamine. However, it has been shown that amphetamine also increases the amount of available dopamine as well, using two mechanisms at the cellular level.

Routes of administration for amphetamines include the oral route, "snorting," and intravenous (IV) route. Absorption by the oral route may take up to 30 minutes for effects to be experienced. Snorting may produce effects in 5 minutes, while IV administration provides rapid effect.

The duration of action of amphetamines lasts from 4 to 6 hours, regardless of the route of administration. The intensity is greater with snorting and IV use, but the drug remains active for the same time frame whether it is taken orally, nasally or injected.

Amphetamine is metabolized by the liver at a slow rate. The half-life of amphetamines can be between 7 and over 30 hours, depending on the rate of metabolism and the pH of the urine.

Street names for amphetamines include *uppers, bennies, dexies, black beauties, diet pills, speed, beans, crosstops, pep pills, christmas trees.* Street prices vary from $5 to $10 per tablet or capsule.

The amphetamine products available are listed in the table below. The extended release versions utilize capsules that contain different types of beads that dissolve at different rates, releasing drug over an extended period of time. Images of the amphetamines may be seen in Appendix 2.

Products

Brand Name	Generic Name	Dosage	Form
Dexedrine	Dextroamphetamine	5mg, 10mg, 15mg	Extended Release Capsule (Spansule)
Dextrostat	Dextroamphetamine	5mg, 10mg	Tablet
Vyvanse	Lisdexamfetamine	20mg, 30mg, 40mg, 50mg, 60mg, 70mg	Capsule
Adderall	Dextroamphetamine mixed salts	5mg, 7.5mg, 10mg, 12.5mg, 20mg, 30mg	Tablet
Adderall	Dextroamphetamine mixed salts	5mg, 10mg, 15mg, 20mg, 25mg, 30mg	Extended Release Capsule

Methamphetamine

Methamphetamine is the methylated form of amphetamine, the chemical addition of a methyl group to the amphetamine compound.

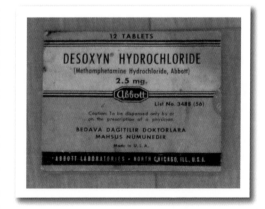

Amphetamine

Methamphetamine

The –CH3, or methyl group at the right end of the molecule, makes the molecule more lipid soluble and able to cross the blood brain barrier more easily and extensively than the amphetamine chemical. The methylated version of the drug is also more stable against enzymes that break the molecule down, thus allowing the drug to remain active in the brain for a longer period of time.

Methamphetamine was first synthesized in Japan in 1919, but did not gain widespread use until the time of World War II. The German military dispensed it to the troops under the trade name Pervitin, and the Japanese military used large amounts of methamphetamine to increase endurance. The 1950's saw the use of the brand name *Desoxyn* and *Methedrine* in the U.S. being prescribed for ADHD, obesity and narcolepsy.

Recreational use of methamphetamine increased during the 1950's and 1960's, mainly used by students and truck drivers to remain awake and alert. The smokeable form of the drug became popular during the late 1960's, and has since become the most popular form for abusing methamphetamine.

Methamphetamine can be taken orally, snorted, smoked, or injected. The crystallized form of the drug burns at a low enough temperature to produce vapors that can be inhaled. The powdered form of the drug is readily soluble in water for preparing an injectable form of the drug. As with all drugs, the route of administration determines the rate at which the drug enters the bloodstream and the brain, and the intensity of the effects of the drug. Methamphetamine being no exception, the smoked and injected route provides extremely large amounts of the drug to the brain in a very short amount of time, producing euphoric effects.

The effects of methamphetamine use include dilated pupils, flush or pale skin, a rapid and/or irregular heartbeat, and fatigue to the point of possible physical collapse after continuous use.

Effects of smoking or injecting methamphetamine are felt within 5 to 10 seconds of administration. Snorting the powder produces effects within 3 to 5 minutes, while oral tablets will take 15 to 20 minutes to begin producing an effect. Thus, smoking and injecting will provide the "rush" that is sought by those using the drug. Snorting and oral use will provide a less intense overall effect. The overall duration of the effects will last from 2 to 5 hours for oral and insufflated (snorted) routes, and 1 to 3 hours for smoked and injected routes.

Methamphetamine

Methamphetamine

Dosages of methamphetamine powder and crystals range greatly, depending on tolerance and route of administration. Doses of only 5mg may be used to produce mild effects in a novice user, while one with considerable tolerance may require doses over 100mg.

As *"crack"* earned its name as a smokeable form of cocaine, the smokeable form of methamphetamine is referred to as *ice, crystal, glass,* or *shards.* This form is of higher purity, and easier to produce. Other street names for methamphetamine include *meth, speed, zip, chalk, and crank.*

Street prices for methamphetamine vary depending on region, purity, and availability. An average price of $100 per gram has been reported, with "ice" crystals selling for over $200 per gram, with fluctuations common.

Production

Methamphetamine production is mainly accomplished through clandestine operations that involve the use of a home laboratory and the process of several chemical reactions.

The chemical reaction necessary to produce methamphetamine is the reduction, or hydrogenation, of pseudoephedrine by addition of anhydrous ammonia and lithium. Anhydrous ammonia, NH3, is usually obtained from agricultural fertilizer. Lithium, Li, is extracted from lithium batteries. The chemical similarity between pseudoephedrine, a common decongestant sold over the counter as Sudafed® and other brands, with methamphetamine makes this process easily done.

Pseudoephedrine   *Methamphetamine*

Noxious fumes and the explosive potential when mixing the reactants make the manufacturing of methamphetamine extremely dangerous, yet very profitable. For approximately $100 worth of ingredients, a product can be produced and sold for over $1,000.

As pseudoephedrine began flying off of the shelves of retailers nationwide, the U.S. DEA enacted the Combat Methamphetamine Act of 2005, to interfere with the purchase of over the counter drugs intended for use in the manufacture of methamphetamine. The act listed pseudoephedrine, ephedrine, and phenylpropanolamine, all OTC drugs used in the process, as regulated items that were now required to have special storage and purchasing provisions. Retailers are required to keep products out of public access, maintain logbooks with purchaser identification, and limit the amounts that may be sold to an individual during a 30 day period, which is 9 grams of pseudoephedrine.

Methamphetamine remains a Schedule II product under the Controlled Substance Act of 1970. It is available as the brand name Desoxyn® in 5mg tablet strength.

Methylphenidate

Commonly known as the popular brand name Ritalin®, methylphenidate is a prescribed stimulant used in the treatment of attention deficit hyperactivity disorder (ADHD). As with the other stimulants discussed, methylphenidate increases neurotransmitters levels of dopamine and norepinephrine in certain areas of the brain. In the case of treating hyperactivity, this would seem paradoxical. However, patients with ADHD have been shown through MRI to have decreased activity in areas related to concentration, thus stimulation results in less hyperactivity.

Methylphenidate

Methamphetamine

There exists a chemical similarity between methylphenidate and methamphetamine, namely the ring structure to the left, and the position of the "N" or nitrogen to the right. Both drugs produce stimulation, lessen fatigue, improve attention, and have the ability to induce euphoria, especially at higher doses. It is at higher doses of the drug that the effects of methylphenidate are sought and the drug is abused.

Tablets of Ritalin® and other methylphenidate formulations are prescribed for adolescents who are diagnosed with ADHD. These tablets are readily available and easily diverted for use as a study aid, a weight loss supplement, or fuel for battling fatigue. The tablets may be taken orally, crushed and snorted, or mixed into solution for IV administration. When administered to an IV cocaine user, IV methylphenidate is reportedly indistinguishable from cocaine. Recreational use of methylphenidate is common in the college environment, as the stimulant ability of the drug assists with the ability to study much more possible than without the drug's influence, or to socialize for many more hours. Street names include *Vitamin R, R-Ball,* and *Smart Drug.* Street prices vary from 50 cents to $5 per tablet.

Methylphenidate chronic use includes adverse effects of nervousness, insomnia, anorexia, nausea, heart palpitations, headache, increased blood pressure, and cardiac arrhythmias. The majority of these effects are seen with use at dosages higher than prescribed.

Methylphenidate is a Schedule II drug under the Controlled Substance Act of 1970, indicating that a high potential for abuse is recognized for this drug. It is available under various names and strengths listed in the table below. Images of the methylphenidate products may be seen in Appendix 2.

Name	Strength	Form
Ritalin	5mg, 10mg, 20mg	Tablet
Ritalin SR	20mg	Controlled Release Tablet
Methylin	5mg, 10mg, 20mg	Tablet
Methylin ER	10mg, 20mg	Controlled Release Tablet
Concerta	18mg, 36mg, 54mg, 72mg	Controlled Release Tablet
Ritalin LA	10mg, 20mg, 30mg, 40mg	Controlled Release Capsule
Metadate CD	10mg, 20mg, 30mg, 40mg, 50mg, 60mg	Controlled Release Capsule
Daytrana	10mg, 15mg, 20mg, 30mg	Controlled Release Patch

Anorectics

Anorectics are drugs prescribed for appetite suppression and weight loss. These drugs are chemically similar to amphetamines, and also have similar pharmacological profiles, as they affect neurotransmitters in the brain, mainly norepinephrine, that decrease appetite. They also produce increased central nervous system activity, which leads to increased heart rate and blood pressure, restlessness and insomnia, as do the amphetamines. Side effects include dry mouth, headache, nervousness and dizziness. Tolerance to the anorectics develops quickly, sometimes within a few weeks of starting therapy. Thus, these drugs are not indicated for use any longer than a period of "up to 12 weeks," as increasing dosages of the medication will be needed. Withdrawal symptoms include fatigue and depression. Anorectics are abused for their stimulant properties, and may be snorted or injected IV, but are mainly taken orally at increased dosages. Viewed by many physicians as having a minimal risk for abuse, anorectics are readily prescribed to patients seeking assistance with diet plans that may or may not be legitimate.

The anorectics listed are Schedule III or IV drugs under the Control Substance Act of 1970, as there is a risk of abuse associated with these medications.

Phentermine

-Fastin, Adipex-P, various generics (37.5mg tablet), twice a day.
-Ionamin (15mg and 30mg capsule), once a day.

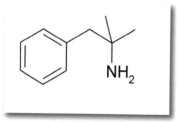

Phentermine

Adipex tablet

Phentermine capsule

Phentermine tablet

Ionamin 30 mg capsule

Ionamin 30 mg capsule

Diethylpropion

-Tenuate, various generics (25mg and 75mg extended-release tablet), once to three times a day.

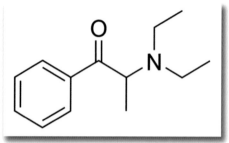

Diethylpropion

Tenuate 25mg tablet

Tenuate 75mg tablet

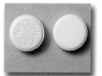

Generic diethylpropion

Sirbutramine

-Meridia (5mg, 10mg and 15mg capsule), once a day

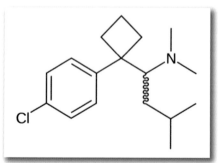

Sirbutramine

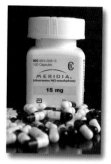
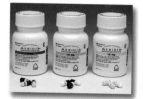

Meridia capsules

Phendimetrazine

-Bontril (35mg tablet), three times a day.

-Prelu-2 (105mg extended-release capsule), once a day.

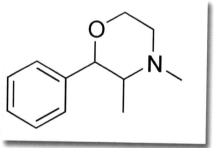

Phendimetrazine

Bontril 35mg tablet   *Bontril 105mg tablet*

Benzphetamine

-Didrex (50mg tablet), one to three times a day.

$$CH_3$$
$$|$$
$$CH_2NCHCH_2$$
$$|$$
$$CH_3$$

· HCl

Benzphetamine

Didrex 50mg tablet

Khat

Khat leaves bundled

Khat is a bush that is native to East Africa and surrounding areas, and grows to produce leaves and flower tops that are chewed or dried for tea, in order to produce stimulating effects. The similarity of drinking a strong cup of coffee has been used when describing the effects of khat. The use of khat has been documented to as far back as 11th century Persia, and was prescribed for maladies of the stomach and liver.

The leaves of the khat bush retain their potency only while fresh, and will decompose after approximately 48 hours. This has led to the confined use of the drug to those areas local to its growth. Improved transportation and shipping methods have, however, allowed the leaves to enter into worldwide markets where immigrant populations have grown.

The main chemical isolated from the khat leaf is a substance known as cathinone, an alkaloid similar in structure to amphetamine.

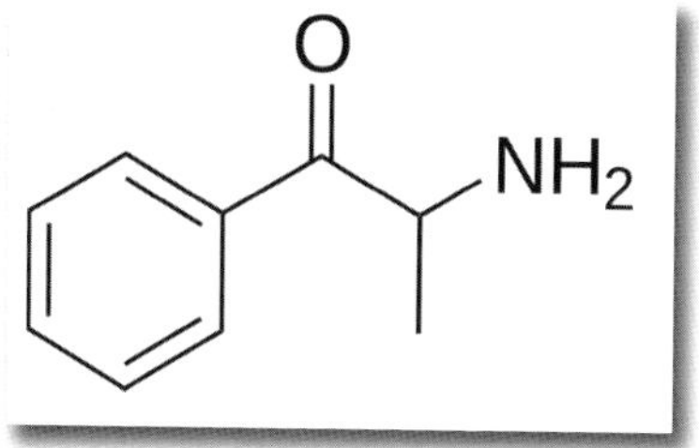

Cathinone

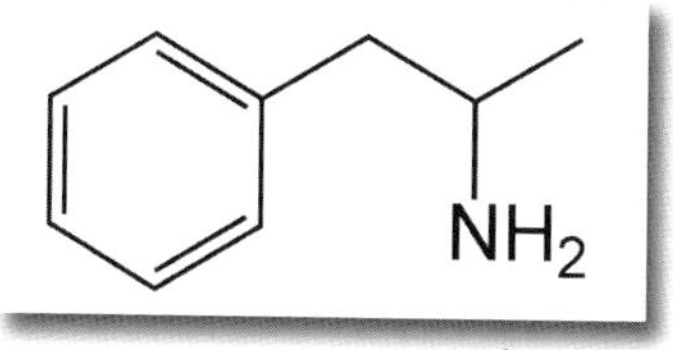

Amphetamine

By chewing the leaves, users experience the stimulating properties associated with khat, including increased energy and decreased fatigue, decreased appetite, increased heart rate and blood pressure, and dilated pupils. The effects are felt within 15 to 30 minutes of chewing, as the drug enters the bloodstream through the mucous membranes of the mouth and stomach. Peak blood levels are reached within 2 hours, and the drug has a half-life of elimination of approximately 4 hours. The leaves are chewed until they become dried, and are then spit out. An average "dose" is between 100 and 200 grams of leaves.

Street names include qat, quat, jaad, mirra, chat, African salad. Street prices have been reported to be $300 per kilogram, with bundles being sold in the $30 to $40 range. Khat has been listed by the U.S. DEA as a Schedule I drug under the Controlled Substance Act of 1970, stating that no medical use exists and a high potential for abuse.

Depressants

The category of drugs known as the depressants include drugs that are used to treat anxiety, which are called *anxiolytics*, also known as *sedative-hypnotics*. These drugs have traditionally been called "downers" in that they produce relaxed, calming, drowsy effects in the user. The two major groups of drugs in this category are barbiturates and benzodiazepines. The history of this category of drugs can be traced through the development of the first barbiturate and the subsequent discovery of the benzodiazepines. Various other sedating drugs will be discussed as well, including such drugs as *flunitrazepam, GHB, quetiapine,* and *carisoprodol.* The anxiolytics are synthetically produced drugs that have been continuously brought to market since the beginning of the 20th century. There is a large market in the U.S. for anxiety and insomnia relief, and sedative-hypnotics constitute a very large share of the prescription market. At higher doses, and in combination with alcohol and other drugs, these drugs provide a relaxed, drowsy state to a user, and are commonly abused. They are also useful as an antidote for abuse of stimulants, and assist in "coming down" from a high when sleep is needed.

"The art of medicine consists in amusing the patient while nature cures the disease"
-Voltaire (1694-1778)

"...The phenomenon outlasts the antianxiety effects of these drugs ...people are seeking an easy way out, looking for shortcuts on the path of life...."
-Dr. Louis Gottschalk, neuroscientist

History

Early twentieth century scientists and medical professionals saw a need for a chemical that would help people relax and sleep, a sedative. This was accomplished initially in 1903 in Germany, as a compound being tested was shown to be effective at putting dogs to sleep. This drug was marketed initially by the Bayer company under the trade name Veronal®, the first barbiturate. Luminal®, trade name for phenobarbital, was introduced in 1912 as an improvement of the original barbiturate. The base chemical of the barbiturate molecule allowed for extensive substitution to create variations of the molecule, and many different drugs. Over 2,500 different chemicals with pharmacological activity were produced, and many were brought to market until the 1950's. The drawbacks of barbiturates, mainly that they were highly addictive, very sedating, toxic, and that abrupt withdrawal could be fatal, led to the need for a safer "tranquilizer." Users would forget how many capsules had been taken, or if any, and would accidently overdose with great frequency. Rapid tolerance to the drug led to subsequent lethal respiratory depression.

Meprobamate, brand name Miltown® was available for use during the 1950's. Unrelated chemically to the barbiturates, it was considerably safer than the barbiturates, but still had problems, including drug interactions, side effects, and over sedation. However, it was a very popular drug during its time and introduced the general public to the term "tranquilizer." The following advertisements tout its many uses.

By the mid-1950's, the term "minor tranquilizer" was offered as the type of drug needed to replace the sedating, toxic effects of the barbiturates and Miltown®. The Hoffman-LaRoche company succeeded in accidentally creating a new chemical entity, the first benzodiazepine, which was named "chlordiazepoxide" or brand name of Librium®. Continued research on the physiological activity of chlordiazepoxide led to the discovery of its main metabolite, diazepam, four years later. Diazepam, or brand name Valium® soon became one of the most prescribed drugs in the U.S. These new drugs offered a safer profile than the barbiturates in terms of toxicity, as the risk of overdose was less. They were capable of reducing anxiety without causing over sedation, exactly the combination of effects needed.

The 1960's and 70's saw the hugely popular drug methaqualone (Quaalude®) being prescribed and abused for its relaxing and euphoric properties. Classified as a CNS depressant, its effects and chemistry were similar to the barbiturates.

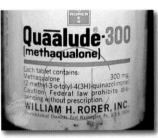

Manufactured by the Rorer and Lemmon companies, the drug number "714" was stamped on the tablets, giving the drug its street name. By 1982, methaqualone was moved to Schedule I in the U.S. and removed from the market, due to the level of abuse of the drug.

Lude/rorer/714

The benzodiazepines were also being marketed and prescribed as *non-addictive,* unlike the former barbiturates. The introduction of alprazolam, brand name Xanax® in the early 1980's solidified the status of benzodiazepines in the drug chest of America.

Additional benzodiazepines were brought to market, as well as several non-benzodiazepine drugs to address the ever growing population in need of anxiety relief. The benzodiazepines are now recognized to cause dependence and abuse, and are Schedule III and IV controlled substances under the Controlled Substance Act of 1970. Physicians have begun to prescribe anti-depressants and other non-controlled drugs to address anxiety relief and insomnia for their patients in addition to benzodiazepines. The use of barbiturates as an anxiolytic or sedative decreased significantly with the introduction of newer drugs.

Barbiturates

The barbiturates were the first drugs used as anxiolytics, and many different types of barbiturates were developed over the years, all variations of the same basic chemical structure. Barbituric acid was the chemical basis that was modified to produce drugs that had different profiles of bioavailability; that is, every modification of barbituric acid produced a chemical that behaved differently in terms of the pharmacokinetic factors of absorption, distribution, and metabolism.

Barbituric acid

By chemical addition of side-chains of varying sizes to the basic molecule, different barbiturates are created that have different chemical properties and capabilities, which accounts for the drugs' pharmacokinetic differences. Lipid solubility is affected by the size and type of side chain, which will determine the onset of effect and duration of action. It is on this basis that barbiturates are classified into three distinct groups: (1) ultrashort-acting (2) short/intermediate-acting (3) long-acting.

1. Ultrashort-acting

The ultrashort-acting barbiturates include thiopental (Pentothal®) and methohexital (Brevital®), sedatives used for intravenous anesthesia.

Thiopental (Pentothal)

The chemical side chain makes thiopental very lipid soluble and readily cross the blood brain barrier to induce sedation very quickly, usually within 10 to 20 seconds. The molecule is broken down very quickly as well, and the duration of the drug's effect may be 20 to 30 minutes. Fast onset of action, short duration of action is the profile for ultrashort-acting barbiturates.

2. Short/intermediate-acting

The short/intermediate-acting barbiturates include amobarbital (Amytal®), secobarbital (Seconal®), and pentobarbital (Nembutal®), oral sedatives useful for surgical anesthesia and sleep induction. Butalbital (Fiorinal®, Fioricet®) is an intermediate acting barbiturate used in combination with aspirin or acetaminophen for treatment of headache and pain.

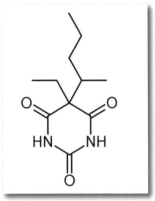

Pentobarbital (Nembutal)

The chemistry of the short/intermediate-acting barbiturates offers moderate lipid solubility, and an onset of action within 20 to 40 minutes. The duration of action may be between 5 and 8 hours. These parameters make the barbiturates of this group well suited for sleep induction, which is what their traditional use has been. This group of barbiturates has also been the drugs that were the most likely to be abused. The following table lists the common street names of the barbiturates.

Barbiturate	Street Name
Pentobarbital (Nembutal)	Abbotts, nembies, yellow bullets, yellow dolls, yellow jackets, yellows
Amobarbital (Amytal)	Blue angels, bluebirds, blue bullets, blue devils, blue dolls, blues
Secobarbital (Seconal)	F-40's, Mexican reds, redbirds, red bullets, red devils, reds
Secobarbital/amobarbital (Tuinal)	Christmas trees, double trouble, gorilla pills, rainbows, tootsies
General	Downers, goofballs, King Kong pills, peanuts, pink ladies, sleepers, softballs

3. Long-acting

The long-acting barbiturates include the drugs phenobarbital (Luminal®) and mephobarbital (Mebaral®), which are used mainly for seizure control and prolonged sedation.

The chemistry of phenobarbital produces a drug that has poor lipid solubility and thus limited perfusion of the blood brain barrier, which results in less sedation, and an onset of action of approximately one hour. However, the drug resists metabolism and remains in the bloodstream for an extended period of time, having a duration of action of 10 to 12 hours. The pharmacokinetic profile of phenobarbital, as well as the discovered anti-seizure activity of the drug, has led to its use exclusively in seizure control and prevention.

Images of the barbiturate products may be seen in Appendix 3.

Phenobarbital

Abuse and Illicit use

The barbiturates were highly abused substances while they were commonly prescribed during the 1950's and 1960's, but are rarely used now by physicians, and are all but unavailable for street use. The capsules were simply taken orally in higher than prescribed dosages, and combined with alcohol to enhance the sedating effect. Capsules of the powder could be opened and the contents dissolved in water to produce a solution for injection, which created an effect in the user similar to heroin. As stated previously, the abuse of the barbiturates, as well as their tendency to cause overdose easily, led to the discovery of the benzodiazepines, which are currently prescribed and abused in large numbers.

Benzodiazepines

The drugs known as the benzodiazepines are used extensively for their ability to relieve anxiety, promote sleep, act as a muscle relaxant, control convulsions, or as a sedative for minor surgical procedures. As with the barbiturates, benzodiazepines are classified according to their pharmacokinetic profile, particularly the duration of action of the drug, which is expressed in terms of half-life. A long half-life, which may be up to 200hrs, constitutes a *long-acting* benzodiazepine. An intermediate half-life, which many range from 10 to 75 hrs, would be an *intermediate-acting* benzodiazepine. A half-life of 2 to 6 hours would define a *short-acting*

benzodiazepine. The differences in the duration of action of these drugs is determined by the method of metabolism, or how the drug is broken down in the body, and the extent to which the drug is distributed into fat deposits for redistribution at a later time. Again, the chemistry of the molecule and the processes that it undergoes in the human body will give the drug its specific characteristics. These characteristics will lend to particular uses for the different benzodiazepines, such as presurgical anesthesia *(short-acting)* or all day anxiety control *(long-acting)*.

All benzodiazepines share a common "core" chemical structure, with side chains added to create different drugs with the different pharmacological properties discussed. This common structure is illustrated below:

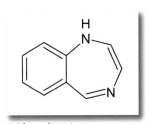

1,4-benzodiazepine

The core structure is comprised of two rings, one a benzene ring (left) and the other a *diazepine* ring (right) which has two nitrogen atoms "N" in the ring. Together, these two rings form a benzo-diazepine. It is that simple. As side chains or substituents are chemically added in specific places on the molecule, different benzodiazepines are created.

Diazepam

Alprazolam

Action, Effects, Tolerance, Withdrawal
Mechanism of Action
All benzodiazepines exert their effects on the natural brain chemical known as GABA (gamma-aminobutyric acid). GABA is the *inhibitory* messenger in the brain, meaning that its message to the neurons that it contacts is to slow down, to transmit less information. Through a complex chemical reaction, GABA reacts with receptors on the neuron cell surface that opens a channel to the cell to an influx of charged particles, making the cell unable to become excited. Benzodiazepines act by enhancing the actions of GABA, making its influence on neurons greater and more extensive throughout the brain.

The brain's normal output of excitatory neurotransmitters such as serotonin and norepinephrine is reduced when GABA production is increased. Alertness, memory, muscle coordination are all affected. This results in the effects that are seen by using benzodiazepines such as drowsiness, dizziness, short-term memory loss, mental confusion, muscle weakness, and lack of coordination.

Effects
Benzodiazepines can produce certain effects that are worth particular mention.
- **Oversedation** - A "hangover" may be experienced the next day when used as a sleeping pill. However, the sedating effects of benzodiazepines usually subside over one to two weeks, as tolerance develops.
- **Drug Interactions** - Additive effects are experienced with other sedating drugs such as opiates and alcohol. Benzodiazepines are frequently found in fatal overdoses.
- **Memory Impairment** - The benzodiazepines cause impairment with short-term or "episodic" memory, which can also manifest as blackouts.

- **Paradoxical Stimulation** - excitement seen as increased anxiety accompanied by insomnia, irritability and aggressive behavior.
- **Depression** - Long term use may cause and aggravate depression, which may be a result of neurotransmitter suppression.

Tolerance

Regular use of benzodiazepines leads to tolerance of the drug, in that more of the drug is needed to produce the desire effects. However, the different effects and actions produced by benzodiazepines develop tolerance at different rates and degrees. Tolerance to the sedating effects develops very quickly, usually within a few weeks. If used for sleep, the benzodiazepines will lose their effectiveness in this short time, and will require a dosage increase. Therefore, they should not be prescribed for any longer than a few weeks for insomnia. Tolerance to the anxiolytic effects of the benzodiazepines takes longer to develop, but will require dosage increases after a few months. Tolerance to the motor effects of the drug develops greatly, and individuals on large doses may not display any decreased level of coordination.

Dependence and Withdrawal

Psychological and physical dependence to benzodiazepines can occur in as little time as a few weeks of taking the drug at therapeutic dosages. Dependence can be determined by examining several different behaviors associated with one's "benzos": Taking the drug for years; a need to take the drug for everyday activities; difficulty stopping or reducing the drug; anxiety regarding the prescription (How many pills left? How many refills?); calling doctor for early refills; carrying pills at all times; increasing dosage at stressful events.

Withdrawal from benzodiazepines can produce severe symptoms, and usually prohibits people from being able to stop taking them. The long-acting nature of the drug requires that withdrawal be accomplished over time with tapered dosages. Abrupt cessation is not recommended.

Withdrawal symptoms will appear after stopping the drug within 24 to 48 hours if one has been taking short-acting benzodiazepines. Symptoms may be delayed for up to 3 weeks if long-acting benzodiazepines were used, as the drug has distributed into body tissue and breaks down much more slowly. The withdrawal period could last between 2 and 12 months. Slow titration (reduction) of the dosage of the benzodiazepine will lessen the likelihood and severity of the symptoms. Protocols and programs exist to address benzodiazepine withdrawal in the best manner for each individual case.

Symptoms of withdrawal include suicidal tendencies, seizures, insomnia, irritability, anxiety, tremor, muscle pain, tingling feelings, gastrointestinal irritation, shaking, and cognitive deficits.

Benzodiazepine Products

The following table includes the most commonly prescribed benzodiazepines. Images of the benzodiazepine products can be seen in Appendix 3.

Generic Name	Brand Name	Classification	Onset of of Action (hrs)	Duration of Action (hrs)	Approx. Dosage
Alprazolam	Xanax	Short	1-2	6-12	0.5 - 1mg
Chlordiazepoxide	Librium	Intermediate	1-4	5-30	25mg
Clonazepam	Klonopin	Intermediate	1-4	18-50	0.5 - 1mg
Clorazepate	Tranxene	Long	Variable	36-100	15mg
Diazepam	Valium	Long	1-2	20-100	5 - 10mg
Estazolam	ProSom	Intermediate	0.5-5	10-24	1 - 2mg
Flurazepam	Dalmane	Long	1-1.5	40-250	15 - 30mg
Lorazepam	Ativan	Short	2-4	10-20	1mg
Midazolam	Versed	Short	0.5-1	2-6	5 - 8mg
Oxazepam	Serax	Short	3-4	4-15	20mg
Temazepam	Restoril	Short	0.5-3	5-20	15 - 30mg
Triazolam	Halcion	Short	0.5-2	2-6	0.25mg

Alprazolam

Sold under the brand name Xanax®, alprazolam is a potent, short-acting benzo used in the treatment of severe anxiety and panic attacks. It is available as an immediate release tablet in strengths of 0.25mg, 0.5mg, 1mg and 2mg. The ER, or extended-release, tablet is available in strengths of 0.5mg, 1mg, 2mg and 3mg. Alprazolam is the most commonly abused benzodiazepine, due to its rapid acting onset of action and availability. It is usually taken orally, as the tablets do not dissolve well in solution for IV use, and snorting the powdered tablet is inefficient as it does not allow enough drug to pass through the nasal membrane.

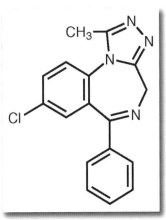

Alprazolam

Alprazolam is known on the street as *zannies, footballs,* or *bars,* as the tablets have a characteristic football shape, and the 2mg tablet is known as a "bar," scored for dosing flexibility. Street price of alprazolam varies for about $1 to $4 per tablet, depending on strength, to up to $8 per 2mg "bar."

Zannie bar

Chlordiazepoxide

Librium® is the trade name for this intermediate-acting benzodiazepine, which is prescribed for short term treatment of anxiety (2 to 4 weeks), and in the medication assisted treatment of acute alcohol withdrawal. It was the first benzodiazepine discovered. It is available in capsules of 5mg, 10mg and 25mg strengths. Street value of chlordiazepoxide is very low, as the drug has a long duration of action and does not have a significantly fast onset of action. It is prescribed rarely and is not readily available. It is useful in the management of the physical symptoms that accompany alcohol withdrawal.

Clonazepam

Clonazepam is considered an intermediate-acting benzo, marketed under the brand name Klonopin® and used for anxiety and panic disorders, as well mania and seizure control. Clonazepam is available as 0.5mg, 1mg and 2mg tablets. The drug is very lipid soluble and readily passes through the blood brain barrier. Clonazepam is considered the second most abused benzo, as the drug is widely prescribed. Referred to as *klonnies* or *pins* on the street, they can be sold for anywhere between $1 and $4 per tablet, depending on region and availability.

Clonazepam

Clorazepate

Sold under the trade name Tranxene®, this long-acting benzo is used in the treatment of anxiety disorders, insomnia, as an anticonvulsant, and as a muscle relaxant. It is available in strengths of 3.75mg, 7.5mg and 15mg tablets or capsules. Low prescribing practices make clorazepate a rarely found drug of abuse, with street values being determined by market availability.

Diazepam

Valium®, at one time one of the most prescribed drugs on the planet, is a long-acting benzodiazepine prescribed for anxiety, insomnia, seizures, muscle spasms, alcohol withdrawal, and to pre-medicate prior to surgical procedures. Diazepam has a rapid onset of action, making it useful for procedures that require mild sedation and to control seizures. It is available in 1mg, 2mg, 5mg and 10mg tablets. A 15mg time-release capsule is also available, brand name Valrelease®. Diazepam is available in oral solutions of 1mg/ml and a more concentrated 5mg/ml. It is also available in a 5mg/ml solution for IV and IM injection. Diazepam is very lipid soluble and crosses the blood brain barrier easily. It also undergoes extensive metabolism in the body and produces active metabolites which contribute to its long half-life.

Street names for diazepam include *candy, downers, blues, vallies* and *tranks.* Prices vary from $2 to $5 per tablet. Diazepam is frequently mixed with alcohol or opiates to intensify the sedating effect. It has been used in these mixtures or "cocktails" as a substitute for heroin when unavailable.

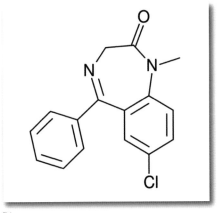

Diazepam

Estazolam

Brand name Prosom®, an intermediate-acting benzodiazepine that is mainly used for the short term treatment of sleep disorders, as it has a rapid onset of action. It is available in 1mg and 2mg tablets. Low prescribing practices limit the availability of estazolam for diversion and misuse.

Flurazepam

Flurazepam, brand name Dalmane® is a long-acting benzo that is prescribed for sleeping disorders. The drug has an onset of action of less than 1 hour, but an extremely long half-life of up to 250 hours. As the drug remains in the body for an extended period of time, next day sedation is common while taking flurazepam at bedtime for sleep. It is available in 15mg and 30mg capsules. The use of other agents for sleep has led to the decline in flurazepam prescriptions and the street supply.

Lorazepam

Lorazepam is a short-acting benzodiazepine that is used in the short term (2 to 4 weeks) treatment of anxiety and insomnia. It is fast acting and useful in treating panic induced anxiety, as it is available as an injectable and oral formulation. Tablets are available as 0.5mg, 1mg and 2mg strengths. The injectable formulations deliver 2mg and 4mg per vial. Street prices reported to be approximately $1 per tablet.

Lorazepam

Midazolam

A short-acting benzodiazepine sold under the brand name Versed®, midazolam is mainly used as to induce sedation prior to medical procedures due to its rapid onset of action and short half-life elimination time. It is available as a 1mg/ml and 5mg/ml injectable. It is the only benzodiazepine that is truly water soluble, making it ideal for an injectable solution.

Midazloam

Oxazepam

Serax® is a short-acting benzo with a slower onset of action, prescribed for individuals who have difficulties staying asleep rather than falling asleep, and for short term treatment of anxiety. It is a chemical that is an active metabolite of other benzodiazepines, namely diazepam and temazepam. It is available in tablets of 10mg, 15mg and 30mg. Oxazepam is not prescribed with great frequency and thus the street availability is low.

Temazepam

A short-acting benzo for the use of maintaining sleep and in treating anxiety, Restoril® was the most prescribed hypnotic in the U.S. during the 1980's. The drug is rapidly absorbed orally, within 30 minutes to produce effects, with an appropriate half-life for addressing sleep disturbances, being on average approximately 9 hours. It is available as a 7.5mg and a 15mg capsule. Known as "jellies" on the street, the gel caps can be dissolved under the tongue for a somewhat faster onset of action. Street prices vary.

Triazolam

A short-acting benzodiazepine marketed under the trade name Halcion®, triazolam is prescribed as a hypnotic in the short-term (7 to 10 day) treatment of insomnia. Its fast onset, as short as 30 minutes, and short half-life of 2 to 6 hours make the drug ideal for users in avoiding morning "hangover." It is available in 0.125mg and 0.25mg tablets. Known on the street as *UpJohns,* after the manufacturer's name, street prices vary. Halcion and generic equivalents of triazolam are not popularly prescribed any longer, and are rare on the street.

Benzodiazepines have been identified as the most popular drug in emergency room reports and in overdose situations. Used alone, benzos have a fairly safe profile and do not pose a fatal overdose risk. It is the effects produced by these drugs when used in combination with other drugs, such as alcohol and opiates that the potential for overdose increases dramatically. The likelihood of respiratory depression becomes much more possible when large quantities of benzos are in the bloodstream along with these other drugs. The use of high doses of benzos to counteract the effects of stimulants can lead to dangerous interactions of the drugs, as the effects are magnified. Polypharmacy, or the use of multiple drugs, has led to the popularity of benzodiazepines, as well as the fatal reporting of these drugs. The sheer availability of many different drugs from different categories manifests in emergency room overdose situations. It is for these reasons that emphasis has been placed on the benzodiazepines in this discussion.

Flunitrazepam

An additional benzodiazepine that must be included in a separate discussion due to
its notoriety and particular use is flunitrazepam, or brand name Rohypnol®.
Originally marketed by the Hoffman-LaRoche company for insomnia, the drug has
a potency of ten times that of diazepam. Rohypnol® is available in 1mg and 2mg
tablets, however, it is not produced or legally sold in the U.S. When mixed with
alcohol, flunitrazepam causes amnesia, blackouts, and a general loss of memory
and disorientation that may last up to 8 hours. Onset of action can be in 30
minutes. It is these sedating characteristics of the drug that have earned it the title
"date rape drug." Odorless, tasteless and colorless when mixed with alcohol,
flunitrazepam can be given to an unsuspecting victim. As with any benzodiazepine,
additive effects are experienced when taken together with alcohol.

Roofies, mind erasers, Mexican valium, R-2, and *forget pill* are some of the names that
refer to Rohypnol. A tablet of flunitrazepam may be purchased illicitly for $5.
Texas, Florida and other southern states have supplies readily available on the street
as the drug is produced in Mexico and imported. Although flunitrazepam is illegal

to produce or obtain in the U.S., it is listed as a Schedule IV drug under the Controlled Substance Act.

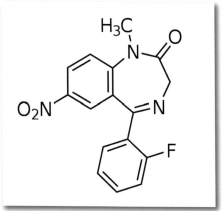

Flunitrazepam

Rohypnol 1mg tablet

Zolpidem

Zolpidem is sold as the brand name drug Ambien®, used in the short term (2 to 6 weeks) treatment of insomnia. It is a chemical that is classified as a non-benzodiazepine, yet its chemical structure is similar to the benzo core:

Benzo core

Zolpidem

Tolerance to zolpidem, dependence and withdrawal symptoms are similar to the benzodiazepines. The usual dose is 5mg or 10mg at bedtime. The drug works quickly, within 15 minutes, to induce sleepiness. Mild euphoria and hallucinations have been reported with the abuse of zolpidem, as well as a "body high" with higher dosages.

Street names for Ambien® include *A-minus* and *Zombie pills* and are sold for $2 to $5 per tablet. The drug is listed as a Schedule IV controlled substance.

GHB

Gamma-hydroxybutyric acid, or GHB, is a CNS depressant that has been used medically as an anesthetic, a hypnotic, and to control narcolepsy. It is chemically unrelated to the barbiturates or the benzodiazepines.

GHB

GHB is illegal in the U.S., a Schedule I drug under the Controlled Substance Act. It can be produced rather easily from two household chemicals gamma-butyrolactone and sodium hydroxide, which are a degreaser and drain cleaner. Amazingly enough, the chemical mixture of these two chemicals produces GHB, a powerful sedative at high doses, and a mildly relaxing drug at lower doses. By influencing levels of serotonin, dopamine, and GABA in the brain, GHB exerts both stimulating and sedating effects, at low and high doses respectively. A complex interaction with the neurotransmitters at varying levels of the drug in the brain will produce the paradoxical results. At low doses, GHB produces effects of euphoria, disinhibition and increased sensuality and sexuality. At higher doses, drowsiness, sedation, amnesia and unconsciousness may result.

The drug is usually available as a clear liquid, or as a white powder. The liquid is transported in small containers, and doses are usually sold as a "capful" for $5 to $25 per cap. The liquid is usually mixed with alcohol, which will produce a potentiated effect. A preparation of the liquid, which is powder dissolved in water, may be difficult to determine in terms of drug concentration. There is no standardization, and a certain "batch" may contain more active drug than another. The standard powder dose is between 1 gram and 3 grams. $50 will buy 100 grams of powder.

Effects of the drug have been compared to alcohol, and usually begin about 10 to 20 minutes after ingestion, and last approximately 2 hours.

Street names of GHB include *G, Liquid X, Liquid Ecstasy, Gamma Oh,* and the use of the drug recreationally is called "G-ing."

Powder/liquid GHB

Quetiapine

A drug that is used as an antipsychotic for bipolar depression, or as a mood stabilizer, quetiapine, or brand name Seroquel® has also been used by physicians to treat insomnia and anxiety. This practice of prescribing drugs for uses other than those recognized is called "off-label" prescribing. The drug is classified as a dopamine and serotonin antagonist, lending to its use as an antidepressant.

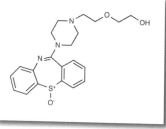

Quetiapine

The dosages of quetiapine for use as a mood stabilizer are between 100 mg and 400mg a day. For panic/anxiety disorders, 25mg to 100mg at bedtime is recommended. For off-label use as a sedative, 25mg to 50mg is taken at bedtime.

Seroquel® is available in tablets of 25mg, 50mg, 100mg, 200mg, 300mg and 400mg. A sustained released version of the drug has become available, Seroquel®XR, in tablet strengths of 50mg, 150mg, 200mg, 300mg and 400mg.

Seroquel has a pronounced side effect of sedation, with inexperienced users of the drug reporting an "out of it" feeling, a desired effect sought by many drug abusers. Since Seroquel is a noncontrolled substance, it is readily prescribed by physicians who may hesitate to prescribe a stronger medication to a patient, particularly one that may be suspect to abuse. The sedating effects of quetiapine make it ideal for "coming down" from stimulant abuse and sleeping off the after- effects that are uncomfortable.

Known on the street as *Q, Qwell* and *Baby Heroin,* quetiapine can be taken orally or crushed and snorted. Dissolving the crushed tablet in water, mixing with cocaine, and injecting the solution, known as a "Q-Ball," has become a common practice. Typically, 400mg to 800mg of quetiapine is mixed with cocaine and injected IV. "Q-balling" is reminiscent of the mixing of heroin and cocaine, known as "speedballing," where a sedating drug and a stimulant are mixed together to augment the effects of each.

Seroquel® tablets usually have a street value of $3 to $5 per 200mg tablet, with larger strengths costing more.

Carisoprodol

A powerful muscle relaxant, carisoprodol was sold under the brand name Soma® for many years, but is now available in a generic form of the drug. The drug is prescribed in the treatment of painful, musculoskeletal conditions, depressing pain signals that reach the brain, and also causing sedation. Its sedating properties are thought to be more valuable than its ability to directly relax muscle, and are used to make a patient feel sedated and to perceive less pain.

Carisoprodol is often prescribed in combination with opiate painkillers in the treatment of injured muscle. Taken alone, the drug has a rapid onset of action with effects lasting between 4 to 6 hours. Taken with an opiate, or a benzodiazepine, or alcohol, the effects of the drug are amplified, with extremely sedating and euphoric effects.

Historically, carisoprodol has not been a controlled substance. This has led to lax physician prescribing practices and the perception that the drug does not have an abuse potential. However, carisoprodol has become a commonly diverted drug available on the street, as those who are prescribed opiates are also prescribed carisoprodol.

Although carisoprodol has not been scheduled as a controlled substance by the DEA under the Controlled Substance Act, several states have enacted stricter regulations and placed the drug in a Schedule IV category within their respective states. An interesting fact regarding carisoprodol is that the drug metabolizes, or breaks down, in the body to a chemical known as meprobamate, which is a drug itself, discussed earlier as the old drug Miltown®. Meprobamate is still available in the generic form, used as a muscle relaxant. However, meprobamate is a Schedule IV drug under the Controlled Substance Act, recognized for its potential for abuse. As carisoprodol is converted to meprobamate in the body, should it be considered a controlled substance as well? Several states have said "yes" to this question, and have recognized the need to control the use of carisoprodol.

Carisoprodol tablets are referred to on the street by the names *D's, SomaComa,* or simply *Soma*. Prices vary by region and availability from $1 to $5 per tablet. Typically used orally alone, or in combination with alcohol, benzodiazepines or opiates.

Hallucinogens

"Reality...what a concept"
-Robin Williams

"I do not do drugs, I am drugs!"
-Salvador Dali

The category of drugs collectively known as hallucinogens are also referred to as *psychedelics* or *dissociatives,* and produce effects that are described as mind-expanding and conscious-altering. Heightened and altered sensory perceptions are the hallmark effects of hallucinogens. Mood, thought and behavior are also affected, with a wide range of effects depending on the individual. The term *"set and setting"* has been used to explain the different experiences among individuals using hallucinogens, referring to the "mindset" of the person and the "social setting" of the experience. Their use has been associated with seeking spiritual and religious meaning, and the cumulative effects likened to meditation and dreams. The experience of certain hallucinogens is referred to as a "trip," since the user seems to leave the daily routine and enter a journey of unexpected and unanticipated experiences. Users may have "good trips" or "bad trips" depending again on the set and setting of the use.

The hallucinogens that will be discussed can be divided into those derived from natural sources and those that are synthetically produced. There exists other chemicals that are used as hallucinogens; however, our discussion will be limited to this particular list of drugs identified by federal agencies involved in treatment and enforcement as the most common. The hallucinogens have all been used either medically or religiously throughout history prior to becoming recreational drugs. Particular histories will be addressed for each drug individually.

HALLUCINOGENS	
Natural	**Synthetic**
Cannabis	LSD
Mescaline	MDMA
Psilocybin	PCP/Ketamine
	Dextromethorphan

Natural Hallucinogens
Cannabis

Marijuana bud

Cannabis, or marijuana, has a long history of use throughout the world, dating back at least 10,000 years. It is currently the most used illicit substance in the U.S. A flowering, weedlike plant with the ability to grow anywhere, *Cannabis sativa* contains more than 60 alkaloid compounds known as *cannabinoids*. The alkaloid "delta-9 tetrahydrocannabinol (THC) is the substance that gives the plant its psychoactive properties.

Marijuana plant

THC

Used throughout Asia, India and Europe from findings dating back to 6,500 B.C. cannabis was eaten, extracted into a "divine nectar," prescribed medicinally, and used socially. The fifteenth century saw the use of *hemp* from the plant, fibers made into rope and sails. Many colonial Americans had hemp farms, including George Washington.

The practice of smoking cannabis began in the U.S. during the late nineteenth century, and became more common shortly after World War I, as Mexican immigrant workers and Caribbean sailors introduced its use in border towns and ports such as New Orleans. As alcohol prohibition was put in place, cannabis use spread quickly and became a popular medicinal and recreational substance until 1937, when a propaganda campaign illustrating the perceived dangers of the drug led to the Marijuana Tax Act of 1937. Use of cannabis became illegal, and all prescribers needed to register for a special stamp to obtain the drug, which was essentially illegal.

The term "marijuana" was given to the plant during the campaign against the drug in the U.S.. It translates from Spanish to mean "intoxicating plant," which was intended to scare people away from using the drug. Marijuana remains illegal under U.S. federal law, being a Schedule I drug under the Controlled Substance Act. However, at the time of this writing, many states have approved its use for medical reasons, and decriminalization of the drug continues to be the ultimate goal for marijuana proponents.

Forms of Cannabis

Cannabis sativa is the species of plant that grows throughout the world and provides the leaves and buds containing the active ingredient THC. Several other species of the plant exist as well, namely *cannabis indica* and *cannabis ruderalis.* Plants can grow to heights of 20 feet, yielding buds that will produce 1/3 to one

pound of product, depending on many factors that include the strain of the plant and the technique used by growers. The buds of the plant contain the most active ingredient, with THC concentrations averaging between 6% and 15%, but able to reach 20%. Sophisticated growing techniques and the development of multiple strains of the plant have led to a very large variety of offerings from the plant, containing varying strengths of THC.

Marijuana bud

The cannabis plant also produces a sticky, concentrated resin that can be collected and pressed into "cakes." This concentrated form of the drug is known as *hash.*

Pharmacology

Delta-9-tetrahydrocannabinol (THC) is a highly lipid soluble substance, and also vaporizes easily when burned, thus it can enter the bloodstream rapidly through the lungs after smoking. Within 20 to 90

Hash

seconds, the drug is able to pass through the blood brain barrier and exert its effects. When ingested orally, the onset of action is usually within 1 hour. Due to its lipid solubility, the half life of marijuana is extended to 20 to 30 hours, although the duration of action of the drug is in the range of 2 to 4 hours.

The discovery of cannabinoid receptors in the brain and other places of the body has helped to explain the effects caused by THC, which is the inhibition of numerous neurotransmitters, including acetylcholine, dopamine, norepinephrine, serotonin and GABA. *Endocannabinoids,* or substances that are endogenous to our bodies, behave like cannabinoids, and interact with cannabinoid receptors, have been discovered throughout the human brain.

Effects and Use
The acute or immediate effects of smoking marijuana include an increased heart rate, dry mouth, reddening of the eyes (expansion of blood vessels), and muscle relaxation. The "high" associated with marijuana use includes feelings of euphoria, relaxation, increased sensitivities and awareness, introspection and creativity; a disruption in linear thinking and perception of time, which is common with the hallucinogens. Motor skills, coordination, and reflexes may be impaired, as is short term memory.

Long term use of marijuana, particularly smoking the drug, may lead to respiratory problems similar to those of tobacco smokers. Marijuana burns and releases up to 70% more carcinogenic substances than does tobacco smoke. Cancer, emphysema and chronic bronchitis become more likely to affect one who has smoked marijuana long term.

Tolerance to the effects of marijuana can develop rapidly, with the use of much larger quantities failing to create the effects experienced initially. Withdrawal from the drug occurs in a more lengthy fashion, as the high lipid solubility of the drug allows the drug to be retained and stored in fat cells, and eliminated much more slowly from the body. Withdrawal symptoms may be delayed in a person for up to several weeks after stopping. These symptoms include irritability, aches, chills, depression, tremor, sleep disturbances, craving, sweating, and loss of appetite.

Marijuana joint

Recreational use of marijuana and hash is predominantly done by smoking the drug. Hand rolled cigarettes known as "joints" or "blunts" contain on average 1 gram of marijuana. The leaves or buds of the plant are broken and placed in a rolling paper (joint) or hollowed out cigar leaf (blunt). A partially smoked joint, like a cigarette "butt," is called a "roach."

Pipes and various smoking devices have been used to smoke marijuana and hash. Pipes, bongs, hookahs, and one-hitters are all used in the burning of marijuana.

One bitter pi

Bong   *Homemade bong*

Street names for marijuana include *pot, herb, grass, weed, bud, dope, ganja, smoke,* and *sens.* Street prices vary based on location and quality of the drug. At the time of this writing, one gram usually sells for around $25 to $30, with a quarter ounce selling for $80 to $100.

Mescaline

Mescaline is a naturally occurring alkaloid found in the peyote cactus of southwestern Texas and central Mexico. The cactus grows with a portion of the plant, the crown, above ground. This crown consists of "buttons" that are cut from the plant and dried. Each button contains 3% to 6% mescaline when dried (less when fresh), and are chewed to ingest the drug.

Peyote cactus

The dose of mescaline is usually 5 buttons which contain between 200 and 500mg of drug. The effects of the drug may last 12 hours, and include psychedelic and spiritual visions, as well as rich visual and auditory hallucinations. Physical effects of the drug include numbness, pupil dilation, increased heart rate, intense nausea and vomiting, and chills and shivering.

The plant has been used for centuries among the Native American Indian tribes for spiritual ceremonies, as well as for its curative properties in various ailments.

The alkaloid mescaline is chemically a phenethylamine, structurally different from other hallucinogens, but similar in structure to amphetamine.

Mescaline

The effects of mescaline are due to the pharmacological processes similar to all of the hallucinogens, which is the complex interference with various neurotransmitters in the brain. The processing of information is changed to such an extent that the sensory input perceived is "filtered" or "channeled" to the cortical regions of the brain via new and different pathways. This disjointed exchange of information in the brain leads to novel perceptions through our senses. "Synesthesia" occurs, which is the crossing of sensory information, such as "hearing a color" or "seeing a song."

The use of mescaline by author Aldous Huxley in 1953 and his reported experience led to the initial interest and popularity of hallucinogens in the U.S. Mescaline is a Schedule I drug under the Controlled Substance Act, with an exception that allows the use in religious ceremonies for certain American Indian tribes. Street names for the drug include *buttons, mesc, peyote* and *mescal.* Mescaline can be extracted from the plant and isolated as a powder, with 500mg providing a dose. Being too large of an amount for packaging as a tablet or capsule, the market for powdered mescaline is not very popular. The natural source of the cactus has also become endangered and rare to find.

Psilocybin

The hallucinogenic drug psilocybin is an alkaloid found in numerous species of mushrooms, which when ingested in the body is converted to *psilocin,* the psychoactive chemical. The practice of ingesting mushrooms can be traced back to 3500 B.C. to use in Algeria, Mexico and Central America. As with mescaline, the use of mushrooms with hallucinogenic properties has been a part of spiritual ceremonies among ancient civilizations such as the Aztec and Mayan. Many different varieties of

Mushrooms

mushrooms exist, with varying potencies of the hallucinogenic drug, each mushroom containing between 3mg and 30mg of psilocybin, mainly in the cap of the plant.

Psilocybin is chemically an indole amine, the prototypical structure of the hallucinogens, which is the two-ring structure with one of the rings containing nitrogen (N). Chemically similar to the neurotransmitter serotonin, the drug exerts its effect on serotonin receptors in the brain.

Psilocybin

Serotonin

The increased effects of serotonin, and other neurotransmitters, after ingesting psilocybin produce acute feelings of lightheadedness, numbness, anxiety, nausea and vomiting, increased heart rate and blood pressure, pupil dilation and dry mouth. Feelings of euphoria, mood swings and visual and perceptual distortions (synesthesia) follow, with the sense of time being altered. Users describe a sense of all boundaries between self and the world dissolve, and a "oneness" exists with everything.

The usual dose of psilocybin is 1 to 5 grams, or 2 to 4 mushrooms. The onset of action occurs within 30 to 45 minutes if the mushrooms are eaten and swallowed. The mushrooms have a bitter taste, and may be taken with other foods to mask the flavor. The mushrooms may also be brewed into a tea. If chewed and held in the mouth, the absorption will take place through the oral mucosa and the effects will be felt within 10 minutes. The duration of action of psilocin is between 2 and 6 hours. The psilocybin alkaloid is metabolized by the liver to psilocin, which enters the bloodstream and the brain.

Mushrooms will only retain freshness for several days, and are usually kept in the refrigerator to preserve. Drying techniques exist to maintain potency for long term storage. Extraction of the alkaloid into a powder is also possible, with the creation of a solution for ingestion.

Magic mushrooms or simply *shrooms* are the street names for the hallucinogenic mushroom. Prices range from approximately $20 for one-eighth oz. to $120 per oz.

Synthentic Hallucinogens
LSD

LSD stands for Lysergic acid diethylamide, a semi synthetic drug produced from lysergic acid found in ergot, a parasitic fungus that grows on rye. A Swiss chemist by the name of Albert Hoffman, working for the Sandoz pharmaceutical company in 1943, accidentally discovered its properties while working on the 25th compound of lysergic acid. Thus, the chemical was referred to as LSD-25. While working with the chemical, Hoffman accidentally ingested a small amount, which he reported in writing:

> *"Last Friday, April 16, 1943, I was forced to interrupt my work in the laboratory in the middle of the afternoon and proceed home, being affected by a remarkable restlessness, combined with a slight dizziness. At home I lay down and sank into a not unpleasant intoxicated-like condition characterized by an extremely stimulated imagination. In a dreamlike state, with eyes closed (I found the daylight to be unpleasantly glaring), I perceived an uninterrupted stream of fantastic pictures, extraordinary shapes with intense, kaleidoscopic play of colors. After some two hours this condition faded away."*

As Hoffman described the first acid trip, his colleagues took some of the LSD-25 as well, confirming his description. The drug was marketed by Sandoz in 1947 under the name Delysid®, for helping in the treatment of neuroses. The drug was distributed in vials containing 25mg of drug. The drug was prescribed at initial doses of 25 *micrograms,* with increases up to 50 to 100 *micrograms.* A microgram is one millionth of a gram. Only a very small amount of LSD-25 was needed to produce profound effects. It is considered the most potent pharmaceutical substance discovered thus far.

Sandoz LSD

Life magazine, 1966

As LSD was being used in psychotherapy during the 1950's, it was also being considered for its potential by the U.S. government, particularly the CIA and a project called MK-ULTRA. The concept of mind control and weaponry were the motivating considerations. The program disbanded not long after it began.

LSD began to be used recreationally during the 1960's, as its mind-expanding abilities seemed to blend well with the anti-establishment culture of the time. The federal government sensed a problem with LSD during this period and in 1965 enacted a law that restricted new research on the drug. Sandoz stopped manufacturing and actually recalled all supplies of the drug on the market. LSD-25 production then became the job of underground chemists, producing the drug in quantities and strengths greater than those seen from Sandoz. LSD was to become the prototype hallucinogen, a symbol of the mind-altering generation that sought to expand the horizons of human existence and experiences. It has become the standard for measuring all hallucinogens, and has undergone extensive research.

Pharmacology

Lysergic acid diethylamide is an indole amine chemical, which is the typical structure of the hallucinogens.

LSD is generally taken by mouth. The effects of LSD usually have an onset of action of 30 to 90 minutes after ingestion. Peak effects occur within 2 to 4 hours, and the effects diminish after 6 to 12 hours. The half-life of the drug is 2.5 to 4 hours. The average dose of LSD is

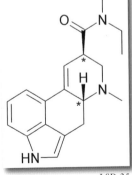

LSD-25

typically 20mcg to 80mcg. During the 1960's, dosages of LSD were seen in the 300mcg to 1000mcg range, over ten times the strength seen in current doses.

Effects include increased heart rate and pressure, dilated pupils, dizziness, loss of appetite, dry mouth. Euphoria, hallucinations, visual and sensory distortions, "synesthesia," as well as a feeling of "egolessness" or "oneness" with the surroundings are the major effects sought after with use of the drug.

Tolerance to the drug's effects will develop if used repeatedly, and higher dosages will be required. There is no evidence of physical dependence, as withdrawal symptoms appear minimal. Drug-induced psychosis resulting in mood swings and depression, as well as the occurrence of "flashbacks" may develop after long term use. A flashback is the experiencing of a subjective episode of a trip long after using the drug.

Use

LSD has been available in several different forms for oral use. Prepared chemically as a liquid, it is distributed by spraying or soaking a particular medium, such as paper or sugar cubes, with the chemical. Sugar cubes were the initial medium used, progressing to a tablet form, and finally blotter paper. Small tablets of LSD were known as *microdots,* as they only needed a small amount of drug to be effective. *Windowpane* contained LSD in a thin gelatin square a quarter of an inch across. Blotter acid was the result of dipping blotter paper into a solution of LSD, water and alcohol for dilution purposes, and soaking the drug solution into the paper. The process may allow for nonstandard distribution of dosages, with some parts of the paper receiving more or less active drug. Individual tabs of paper are distributed as "hits." These papers allowed for elaborate artwork to be displayed, becoming the identifying means naming the batch of drug. The "tab" of paper is simply placed on the tongue and the drug absorbed, with the paper being swallowed eventually.

Blotter hit of LSD   *Blotter LSD*

LSD has had many street names over the years, acid being the most commonly used. *Blotter, microdot, pane, doses* and *trips,* as well as the name of the picture on the blotter paper have all been used to refer to LSD-25. Street prices for acid can be between $3 and $20 per hit. LSD is a Schedule I drug under the Controlled Substance Act.

MDMA

Methylenedioxy-methamphetamine is the drug name for MDMA, a chemical substance related to the amphetamines, but possessing psychoactive properties, it is being classified as a hallucinogen for discussion purposes. It is commonly referred to as "Ecstasy" by those who use the drug. Originally synthesized in 1912 by the Merck company, the drug was never utilized and largely forgotten until 1958, when a Japanese scientist published papers describing the synthesis of the drug.

The therapeutic use of MDMA was popularized by Alexander Shulgin, David Nichols and Leo Zeff beginning in 1978, who published works and touted the drug's value in psychotherapy. The drug enhanced communication among patients in clinical sessions, and seemed to allow those participating to become less inhibited and less defensive, and allow for more therapeutic introspection.

While the medical community was seeking to legitimize the use of MDMA in the psychiatric field, recreational use of the drug started in the 1970's and became prominent in the 1980's, especially in the U.S. MDMA became the drug of choice in dance clubs, known as "raves," as it provided users with energy, euphoria, stimulation and shedding of inhibitions. Its quick rise in popularity, coupled with reports of neurotoxicity, led to the DEA classification of MDMA as a Schedule I drug in 1984, despite the medical community's efforts for legitimate use. The production of MDMA is done illicitly, and brought the term "designer drugs" to popular culture.

Pharmacology

The chemical structure of methylenedioxy-methamphetamine is a blend of amphetamine and the hallucinogen mescaline. The "dioxy" part of the name refers to the two (di-) oxygen atoms (O) attached to left end of the chemical. This portion of the drug changes its activity drastically from that of amphetamine. Norepinephrine, dopamine and serotonin neurotransmitter systems are affected by MDMA.

MDMA

Amphetamine

Mescaline

The drug is absorbed well after oral administration, with an onset of action ranging from 30 to 90 minutes, with peak effects experienced 2 to 3 hours after ingestion. MDMA has a half-life of approximately 8 hours, with metabolites of the drug being active and lingering effects common.

The effects of the drug include increase in body temperature, which may lead to hyperthermia. Users of the drug must drink plenty of water to prevent dehydration, especially if use is accompanied by long periods of activity (dancing). Increases in heart rate, muscle tension and nervousness accompany use of MDMA. Nausea and vomiting, rapid eye movement, headache, dizziness, insomnia and loss of appetite may occur as well. The effects of the drug that are sought by users include euphoria, feelings of comfort, belonging and love, inner peace, awareness and sensitivity to the senses (music), and an overall mood uplifting experience.

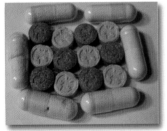

Ecstasy Tablets

MDMA is supplied as tablets of "ecstasy," containing on average 50mg to 100mg per tablet. As with any clandestinely produced drug, amounts and ingredients may not be standardized. Higher dosages may be contained in one tablet, as well as another drug, such as amphetamine, LSD or other substance that mimics the sought effects.

Tolerance to MDMA develops, as experienced users will take several tablets at a time, crush and snort the powder, as well as use IV. Many users will "boost" during the experience with an additional dose. The neurotoxicity of the drug and the increasing damage done to brain tissue may explain why long time users require more of the drug to experience similar effects. Physical dependence may develop, as withdrawal symptoms of fatigue, depression, loss of appetite and difficulty with concentrating are experienced after use of the drug.

Overdose is a real concern with MDMA use, as the body may experience hyperthermia while using the drug. Kidney failure, accompanied by increased blood pressure may lead to loss of consciousness and death. Underlying medical conditions may lend to dangers with MDMA use, as well as disregard for body condition signals such as dizziness, muscle cramping and feeling exhausted, all signs of dehydration.

MDMA has many names on the street, principally "E," "X," *ecstasy, XTC, Adam, biscuits, doves, hug drug.* Typical street prices range from $10 to $40 per tablet, but are usually found in the $20 to $30 per tablet range.

Rave

Ketamine and PCP

The drugs ketamine and phencyclidine (PCP) are presented together as "dissociative" hallucinogens, as their use as anesthetics produce effects described as detachment from the body. PCP was introduced in the mid 1950's as the brand name drug Sernyl® for use in anesthesia. However, during use the drug produced unwanted effects on patients including hallucinations, agitation, and violent behavior. Ketamine was the alternative to PCP, causing less serious effects and having a shorter duration of action. PCP use was replaced by ketamine in the 1960's, and is still available for use in anesthesia.

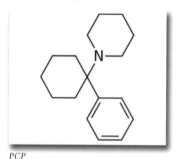

PCP

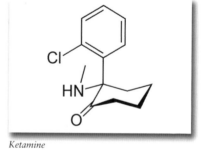

Ketamine

The pharmacological effects of the dissociative drugs are due to inhibition and antagonism of the NMDA (N-Methyl D-Aspartate) receptor, which is widely distributed in the brain. Disruption of the NMDA receptor leads to effects of amnesia, confusion, agitation, mood alteration, as well as nausea, sedation, hypertension and respiratory depression. Sensations of floating and out of body feelings, distortions of shapes, loss of sense of time, visions, and altered perceptions of body and its consistency all are descriptions of effects experienced by PCP and ketamine users.

PCP

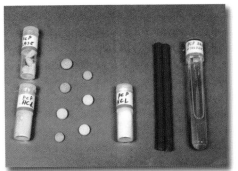

Various forms of PCP

PCP is available in both powder and liquid forms. The powder may be snorted or dissolved for IV use. The liquid form is used for spraying material such as marijuana prior to smoking, or for dipping a cigarette or joint. "Getting wet" or just "wet" refers to this practice, and produces a "dipper."

The powder form of PCP has been historically referred to as "angel dust," which is snorted or smoked with marijuana or tobacco. The liquid has also been called "embalming fluid," probably because of the effects produced being similar to perceived actions that embalming fluid (formaldehyde) may have. PCP is not embalming fluid.

Dosages of PCP can be between 5 and 10mg, with a rapid onset of action, usually between 2 and 20 minutes depending upon route of administration. Peak effects are felt within 2 to 3 hours and the duration of the drug's action is 4 to 6 hours.

Violent and self-injurious behaviors have occurred in those who have had toxic doses of PCP, which happens inadvertently as PCP may be used as a substitute for another drug, producing panic in an unsuspecting user. Convulsions and coma have been reported as well from PCP use.

Angel dust, hog, stupid drug, ozone, rocket fuel, wack, wet or *embalming fluid* is most commonly sold on the street in powder or liquid form, although tablets have been made and available. Street prices include $20 to $30 per gram of powder, $200 to $300 per oz of liquid, and $10 to $20 for a "dipper."

Ketamine

Ketamine powder

Ketamine is available for use in either a liquid or powder form, crystalline powder that is similar in appearance to cocaine. The powdered form is obtained by drying off the liquid portion of the injection solution. The liquid form is available commercially for IV or IM use an anesthetic.

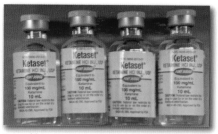

Injectable

The powder form is usually snorted with the apparatus shown known as a "bullet," designed to deliver a specific amount. Doses of 25mg to 50mg are used to deliver a significant effect, with "bumps" of powder measuring the proper amount. The powder may also be added to marijuana or tobacco and smoked, similar to PCP, although the degree of vaporization of the drug may not provide proper burning. Oral ingestion of the powder is also possible, but the effects of the drug are diminished greatly, and only make the user sleepy. The solution for injection is intended to be administered IM (intramuscularly), and not recommended to be used IV (intravenously) as the effects of the drug are felt extremely rapidly and of such an intense nature as to cause dangerous behaviors. Dosages of 25mg to 50mg are considered common, with 75mg to 100mg considered a strong dose. At higher dosages, the user may experience the complete out of body sensation referred to as being in the "K-Hole."

Effects are felt within 5 to 10 minutes of snorting and less than 5 minutes by IM injection. The duration of action of ketamine is relatively short at approximately one hour.

Other effects on the body of ketamine include an increase in heart rate and a decrease in respiration, thus combining with other respiratory depressants such as opiates and alcohol may be fatal. Nausea and vomiting, slurred speech and paralysis occur frequently as well.

Street names of ketamine include *K, Special K, vitamin K* or *cat valium*. Most available ketamine on the street has been diverted from legitimate sources of the drug, mainly veterinarians who utilize ketamine IV solution in practice. A 10ml vial of ketamine can be "dryed off" to produce one gram of powdered ketamine, and be sold for approximately $100. Additives to the yield will increase the volume and profitability. Typical packaging on the street will include 100mg to 200mg and sell for $20.

Dextromethorphan
Introduced as an OTC tablet in the 1960's, dextromethorphan or the brand name Romilar® was used as a cough suppressant in place of the highly sedating codeine. After a period of great sales and high abuse, Romilar tablets were removed from

the market and replaced by the syrup form of the drug. Currently, dextromethorphan is available in many different syrup or capsule cough and cold products, including Robitussin DM, Coricidin Cough and Cold, and various store brand products.

The OTC products contain dextromethorphan (DXM) in combination with other ingredients to address additional symptoms as well as discourage abuse. Guaifenesin is added as an expectorant, but causes nausea, especially at higher dosages. Chlorpheniramine, an antihistamine, and acetaminophen are additional ingredients placed in these products, that may cause kidney and liver damage and even seizures at high dosages.

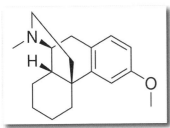

Dextromethorphan

DXM is classified as an antitussive, or cough suppressant, and acts centrally in the brain to suppress the cough reflex. It is chemically related to the opiate class of drugs, and is a semi synthetic derivative of levorphanol, an opiate analgesic. Indicated for cough suppression, the adult dose is 15mg to 30mg three or four times a day. Higher doses allow for NMDA receptor antagonism, a similar process seen with dissociative drugs.

When abused, DXM is taken orally in doses ranging from 100mg to 1500mg. The cough syrup has a concentration of 10mg per 5ml (teaspoonful). Therefore, abuse is taking anywhere from 50ml (10 teaspoonfuls) to 750ml (150 teaspoonfuls), the equivalent of 25 oz., or three 8 oz. bottles.

DXM is abused at high dosages to produce effects of euphoria and visual and auditory hallucinations, as well as dissociation and dreamlike experiences. Other effects include pupil dilation, disorientation, skin sensitivity, loss of coordination, loss of appetite, body itching, dizziness, fever and increased heart rate. Certain effects seem dose-dependent, as hallucinations are associated with dosages over 200mg, and dissociation occurs with dosages greater than 500mg.

Onset of action of the drug occurs in about 20 minutes to 1 hour, with higher dosages taking longer. Effects may have a duration of between 4 to 6 hours. Tolerance develops in those taking higher doses of the drug, and symptoms of withdrawal occur that include anxiety, restlessness, insomnia, diarrhea and vomiting.

Dextromethorphan is available without a prescription in the U.S., and is thus not a controlled substance. It is readily available for purchase and is favored among the adolescent age group due to its easy availability. The drug has street names such as *Triple C* for Coricidin Cough and Cold®, or *Robo Tripping* referring to Robitussin® brand cough syrup. Other names include *skittling, tussin* and *dex.* Street prices reflect the retail price.

Miscellaneous Hallucinogens
These drugs are normally referred to by their shortened chemical names and are sold commercially via the internet. Prices vary, as do DEA regulations governing these chemicals. As they are discovered and monitored, many are eventually placed in Schedule I which severely limits their use. The newer hallucinogens may be synthetic or of a natural source, and can be quite potent requiring very small doses.

5-MeO-AMT
-5-methoxy-alpha-methyltryptamine, "Alpha-O"

5-MeO-DMT
-5-methoxy-dimethyltryptamine

2C-B
-4-bromo-2,5-dimethoxyphenethylamine, "Nexus"

STP
-2,5-dimethoxy-4-methyl-amphetamine

K2
-1-pentyl-3-(1-naphthoyl)indole, also known as JWH-018

Case Studies

The following information was gathered from clients interviewed by the author during the course of their treatment for various drug addictions. Each client was told of the author's intentions of including their stories in this book, and each enthusiastically agreed to participate and have their words reproduced.

*TD

TD entered treatment for an addiction to prescription opiate tablets that had been going on for more than twenty years. TD is currently in his early fifties, is working, and believes that his treatment has saved his life. He feels productive, grateful, and sometimes cannot believe what he has been through. When asked to provide his story for this book, he was more than glad to share his story, as well as the hope that one can get their life back together after many, many years of drug abuse.

TD was a high school athlete, never experimented with drugs, drank alcohol in moderation, and considered himself a "jock." Life after high school included attending college and participating in college football, a passion of his and his family. An injury cut his career short, and college for simply academics did not hold his interest. He returned home and began working for a local businessman, making decent wages with the promise of advancement and a career. As time passed, the advancement did not materialize, and TD became somewhat concerned about his future. During this time period, TD, in his early twenties, had the opportunity to take a pain pill that a friend had, to help with some of his aches and pains. According to TD's recollection, it was euphoria at first dose. To this day, he can recall that day and the feeling that the drug provided him. He recalls asking his friend for more, never taking too many, but enjoying those feelings that he had never experienced before, and was getting very comfortable with now.

As employment and plans fizzled out, TD's use of Percocets did not, and he found himself taking the tablets every day. His career path led him to move to Florida, where he found a good job, a decent place to live, and seemed to be heading in the right direction. He also found himself using his old football injury to persuade doctors to write prescriptions for him for pain pills. TD began taking large quantities of pain medication each day, as much as 15 Percocet tablets a day. A prescription for 80 tablets would last him approximately 5 days. He also found himself getting very good at "the chase," the practice of finding doctors and scoring a prescription. TD states that in over 500 visits to doctor's offices and ER departments, he may have been turned down twice. He relished in "the chase" and recalls getting a high from scoring the pills as well as taking them. He describes the use of opiates over a ten year period as "trying to recapture that first high."

However, the medicine began to lose its effectiveness over time. "The chase" became a necessity, to bring home the medicine to prevent withdrawal symptoms, as he had a job to do daily and could not afford to be sick. TD recalls stressful nights thinking of only one thing: getting a supply for the next day, immediately.

TD places the turning point in his addiction to a time shortly after he had inherited a sum of 12 thousand dollars from a deceased relative. He was never happier, as he figured that he had the money for an endless supply of pills. He can still remember the feeling when he made a $200 withdrawal one night, a mere 2 months after getting the inheritance, an seeing his balance to be $40. He had gone through all of that money! He was terrified. The scope of his problem hit him very hard in that moment and he realized that he had to do something.

He was soon on his way back home to confront his problems and confide in his family. He decided that he needed treatment, and with the blessings and help of his family, he received it. That was nearly 5 years ago, and TD remains in treatment and has not returned to abusing opiates again. He talks about many years lost in a haze of drug seeking and using, and that he would have never thought that he would have been that guy using drugs. However, he now feels thankful for a lot of things and a lot of people in his life.

*JM

JM will tell you all about smoking crack cocaine. She can tell you that she will be smoking some as soon as she can get some, and will probably be smoking all night long. She will tell you how much she loves it, and you can see the mischievous smile on her face and sparkle in her eye. At other times, she will tell you how much she wants to quit using cocaine, how she hates what it does to her and how it can ruin your life. You can see the tears well up in her eyes and the sadness overcome her face.

JM has been using cocaine for 20 years, since she was fourteen years old and attending parties with other school friends. Initially she tried snorting powder, and recalls immediately liking the feeling from the drug. She states that she liked the feeling of sneaking off and doing something that was different from what the others were doing. At the age of sixteen, she tried smoking crack cocaine for the first time. Her recollection now is one of not liking it at first, but soon came to love the feeling that came with smoking cocaine. She has been smoking crack cocaine ever since, usually on a daily basis. She reports periods of smoking crack for 3 and 4 day binges, not stopping to sleep or eat much, and finally collapsing from exhaustion and sleeping for 2 days.

JM does not work, and has lived with her mother for most of her adult life. She states the she will sell portions of her mother's pain medication for money to purchase crack, or will seek any other funding available for crack purchases. She does not mention any issues regarding access to the drug.

She has been using many different sedatives to help her get to sleep after using cocaine, and admits to abusing these drugs frequently, as she needs to offset the effects of large amounts of cocaine. She states that the market for illicit use of depressants and opiates is great simply because of the abuse of cocaine and other stimulants.

JM has said that she feels that she has missed a lot in life because of her cocaine use. She misses family and perhaps opportunities that are no longer available for her. In quiet, reflective moments, she becomes sad about what years of coke use have done, and becomes determined to try to slow down and stop. However, she is never able to maintain that determination for very long, and will inevitably use cocaine on a fairly consistent basis. She acknowledges her frustration, but also seems to come to some realization that using cocaine is one of the few joys that she is able to experience, and that she is comfortable only in the crowds that continue to use cocaine. It is a pattern that began twenty years ago, and continues for her now.

*KK

KK has used many different drugs in his life; from alcohol to opiates, cocaine and depressants. He will talk about how he abused each type of drug for many years, and how he has always been able to stop using once he set his mind to it, grew tired of the drug, or simply did not like it anymore. He is currently in his fifties, and his life has led him to a point where he lives with anxiety on a daily basis; anxiety that, according to him, comes from many sources, including his history of alcohol and drug abuse. His need to seek treatment for his anxiety led him to the use of benzodiazepines, mainly alprazolam and clonazepam, Xanax and Klonopin respectively.

KK will tell you of being introduced to benzos, as they are affectionately called by those who use them. Benzos are highly visible and available on the street and throughout the drug using culture, and KK often found them coming to him when he was using other drugs. The use of these depressants with alcohol and opiates was quite common, and he found himself trying them on occasion. When cocaine was the drug of choice, a benzo would go very nicely with the end of the evening to help him "wind down" and eventually get some sleep. While in the midst of using other drugs, KK developed a relationship and knowledge of the benzodiazepine drugs and their capabilities.

He will also tell you of the terrible withdrawal symptoms he has endured when he has been without any benzodiazepines, or when he has tried to stop taking them on his own, or when his doctor decided that he was no longer going to prescribe them for him. Nausea and vomiting followed by intense headaches, with complete insomnia by the second night, all of a magnitude that becomes unbearable. KK states that he begins to have panic attacks soon afterward, as well as complete sleep deprivation until he can take something to help him.

He continues to be prescribed a benzodiazepine, and reports using them appropriately as prescribed. He no longer abuses the drug, as he no longer abuses other drugs. He feels that he is like so many others who have started taking a benzo by their own means or prescribed by a doctor, that it is unlikely that he will be able to survive without taking the drug. He has learned to use the drug properly, and to resist giving any to others that he knows; "doing them a favor" in his words. KK has seen too many people lightly regard the benzos and use them without realizing the risk involved. In his opinion, it has been the most difficult drug to live with and especially without.

*JB

JB has reached his late forties, and has smoked marijuana since he was fourteen years old. He has dabbled with many other drugs, but has since abandoned all other substances, including alcohol for many years. Yet, he continues to smoke marijuana nearly on a daily basis. He will emotionally defend the drug, claiming that it should not be illegal, has medical benefits, and has helped him cope with many different situations throughout his life. His personal stance on marijuana is certainly shared by many others, and the use of marijuana continues to be commonplace throughout the world. JB and the many users of marijuana will discuss the drug's benefits, stating that it helps one to relax, to socialize, and to enjoy a great many activities while under the drug's effects. Those effects are perceived as being quite benign when compared to alcohol and many other recreational drugs.

Users of marijuana, like JB, will normally have jobs; will not abuse other drugs, and will generally be productive members of society. Listening to JB, one would get the impression that marijuana is a profoundly beneficial substance with no ill effects to discuss.

With the withdrawal effects of marijuana being subtle and lengthy, JB has never really felt any effects related to withdrawal as he usually smokes the drug every day. He claims that the effects of the drug accentuate his daily routine, rather than interfere with his activities. His social circles contain others who share his appreciation of marijuana, and most gatherings include use of the drug.

Appendix 1

Opiate Products

Pharmacokinetic Profiles of Common Opiates
(Compared with Morphine 10MG IM Dose)

DRUG	IM DOSE MG	PO DOSE MG	HALF LIFE HRS	DURATION HRS
Codeine	130	200	2-3	2-4
Oxycodone	15	20-30	2-3	2-4
Morphine	10	30	2-3	3-4
Hydromorphone	2-3	7.5	2-3	2-4
Methadone	1-3	2-6	15-190	4-8
Meperidine	75	300	2-3	2-4
Oxymorphone	1	10	2-3	3-4
Fentanyl	17MCG	17MCG	7	48-72

Opiate Withdrawal Profile

DRUG	Time for Effects to Wear Off	Onset of Withdrawal	Peak of Withdrawal	End of Withdrawal
Fentanyl	1 hr.	3-5 hr.	8-12 hr.	4-5 days
Meperidine	2-3 hr.	4-6 hr.	8-12 hr.	4-5 days
Oxycodone	3-6 hr.	8-12 hr.	36-72 hr.	7-10 days
Hydromorphone	4-5 hr.	4-5 hr.	36-72 hr.	7-10 days
Heroin	4 hr.	8-12 hr.	36-72 hr.	7-10 days
Morphine	4-5 hr.	8-12 hr.	36-72 hr.	7-10 days
Codeine	4 hr.	8-12 hr.	36-72 hr.	7-10 days
Hydrocodone	4-8 hr.	8-12 hr.	36-72 hr.	7-10 days
Methadone	8-12 hr.	36-72 hr.	96-144 hr.	14-21 days

Avinza
30 mg capsule

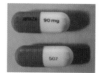

Avinza
90 mg capsule

Avinza
120 mg capsule

Darvocet-N
100 mg tablet

Demerol
50 mg tablet

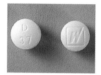

Demerol
100 mg tablet

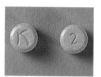

Dilaudid
2 mg tablet

Dilaudid
4 mg tablet

Endocet
5 mg tablet

Endocet
7.5 mg tablet

Endocet
10 mg tablet

Fentanyl
75 mcg patch

Hydrocodone
5 mg tablet

Hydrocodone
7.5 mg tablet

Hydrocodone
10 mg tablet

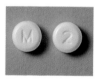

Hydromorphone
2 mg tablet

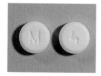

Hydromorphone
4 mg tablet

Hydromorphone
8 mg tablet

Kadian
50 mg capsule

Kadian
60 mg capsule

Kadian
100 mg capsule

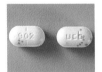

Lortab
5 mg tablet

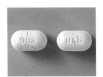

Lortab
7.5 mg tablet

Lortab
10 mg tablet

Meperidine
50 mg tablet

Methadone
5 mg tablet

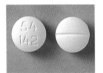

Methadone
10 mg tablet

Morphine Sulfate
15 mg tablet

Morphine Sulfate
30 mg tablet

MS Contin
15 mg tablet

MS Contin
30 mg tablet

MS Contin
100 mg tablet

MS Contin
200 mg tablet

Norco
7.5 mg tablet

Norco
10 mg tablet

Opana ER
10 mg tablet

Opana ER
20 mg tablet

Opana ER
30 mg tablet

Opana ER
40 mg tablet

Oxycontin
10 mg tablet

Oxycontin
20 mg tablet

Oxycontin
30 mg tablet

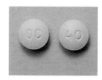

Oxycontin
40 mg tablet

Oxycontin
60 mg tablet

Oxycontin
80 mg tablet

Oxycontin
160 mg tablet

Percocet
5 mg tablet

Percocet
7.5 mg tablet

Percocet
10 mg tablet

Propoxyphene
tablet

Roxicodone
15 mg tablet

Roxicodone
30 mg tablet

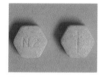

Suboxone
2 mg tablet

Suboxone
8 mg tablet

Tramadol
50 mg tablet

Tramadol
100 mg tablet

Tylenol with codeine
15 mg tablet

Tylenol with codeine
30 mg tablet

Tylenol with codeine
60 mg tablet

Ultram
tablet

Vicodin
5 mg tablet

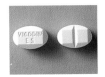

Vicodin ES
7.5 mg tablet

Vicodin HP
10 mg tablet

Vicoprofen
7.5 mg tablet

Appendix 2

Stimulant Products

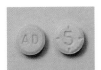

Adderall
5 mg tablet

Adderall
7.5 mg tablet

Adderall
10 mg tablet

Adderall
12.5 mg tablet

Adderall
20 mg tablet

Adderall
30 mg tablet

Adderall XR
10 mg capsule

Adderall XR
20 mg capsule

Adderall XR
30 mg capsule

Amphetamine Salts
5 mg tablet

Amphetamine Salts
7.5 mg tablet

Amphetamine Salts
10 mg tablet

Amphetamine Salts
12.5 mg tablet

Amphetamine Salts
20 mg tablet

Concerta
27 mg tablet

Concerta
36 mg tablet

Daytrana
patch

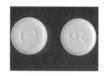

Desoxyn
5 mg tablet

Dexedrine
5 mg capsule

Dexedrine
5 mg tablet

Dexedrine
10 mg capsule

Dexedrine
15 mg capsule

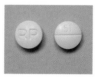

Dextrostat
5 mg tablet

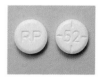

Dextrostat
10 mg tablet

Metadate CD
10 mg capsule

Metadate CD
20 mg capsule

Metadate CD
30 mg capsule

Metadate CD
40 mg capsule

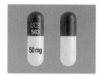

Metadate CD
50 mg capsule

Metadate CD
60 mg capsule

Methylin
5 mg tablet

Methylin
10 mg tablet

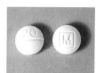

Methylin
20 mg tablet

Methylin ER
10 mg tablet

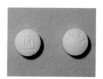

Methylin ER
20 mg tablet

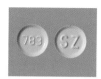

Methylphenidate
5 mg tablet

Methylphenidate
10 mg tablet

Methylphenidate
20 mg tablet

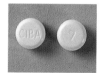

Ritalin
5 mg tablet

Ritalin
10 mg tablet

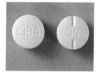

Ritalin
20 mg tablet

Ritalin LA
20 mg capsule

Ritalin LA
30 mg capsule

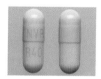

Ritalin LA
40 mg capsule

Ritalin SR
20 mg tablet

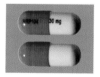

Vyvanse
30 mg capsule

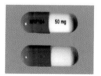

Vyvanse
50 mg capsule

Vyvanse
70 mg capsule

Appendix 3

Depressant Products

Alprazolam
0.25 mg tablet

Alprazolam
0.25 mg tablet

Alprazolam
0.25 mg tablet

Alprazolam
0.5 mg tablet

Alprazolam
0.5 mg tablet

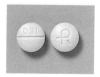
Alprazolam
1 mg tablet

Alprazolam
1 mg tablet

Alprazolam
1 mg tablet

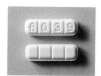
Alprazolam
2 mg tablet

Alprazolam
2 mg tablet

Alprazolam ER
0.5 mg tablet

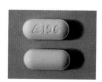
Alprazolam ER
1 mg tablet

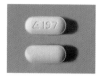

Alprazolam ER
2 mg tablet

Alprazolam ER
3 mg tablet

Ambien
5 and 10 mg tablet

Amytal
200 mg capsule

Ativan
0.5 mg tablet

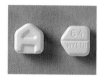

Ativan
1 mg tablet

Ativan
2 mg tablet

Butalbital
tablet

**Butalbital
with codeine**
capsule

Chlordiazepoxide
5 mg capsule

Chlordiazepoxide
10 mg capsule

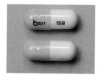

Chlordiazepoxide
25 mg capsule

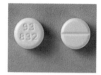

Clonazepam
0.5 mg tablet

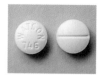

Clonazepam
0.5 mg tablet

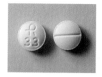

Clonazepam
0.5 mg tablet

Clonazepam
0.5 mg tablet

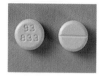

Clonazepam
1 mg tablet

Clonazepam
1 mg tablet

Clonazepam
1 mg tablet

Clonazepam
1 mg tablet

Clonazepam
1 mg tablet

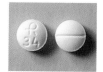

Clonazepam
1 mg tablet

Clonazepam
1 mg tablet

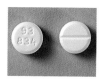

Clonazepam
2 mg tablet

Clonazepam
2 mg tablet

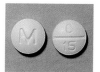

Clonazepam
2 mg tablet

Clonazepam
2 mg tablet

Clorazepate
3.75 mg tablet

Clorazepate
3.75 mg tablet

Clorazepate
7.5 mg tablet

Clorazepate
7.5 mg tablet

Clorazepate
15 mg tablet

Clorazepate
15 mg tablet

Dalmane
15 mg capsule

Dalmane
30 mg capsule

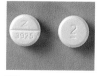

Diazepam
2 mg tablet

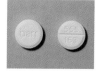

Diazepam
2 mg tablet

Diazepam
5 mg tablet

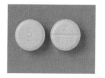

Diazepam
5 mg tablet

Diazepam
5 mg tablet

Diazepam
5 mg tablet

Diazepam
5 mg tablet

Diazepam
10 mg tablet

Diazepam
10 mg tablet

Diazepam
10 mg tablet

Diazepam
10 mg tablet

Estazolam
1 mg tablet

Estazolam
2 mg tablet

Fioricet
tablet

Fioricet with
codeine
capsule

Flurazepam
15 mg capsule

Flurazepam
30 mg capsule

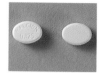

Halcion
0.125 mg tablet

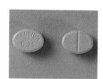

Halcion
0.25 mg tablet

Klonopin
0.5 mg tablet

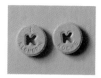

Klonopin
1 mg tablet

Klonopin
1 mg wafer

Klonopin
2 mg tablet

Librium
5 mg capsule

Librium
10 mg capsule

Librium
25 mg capsule

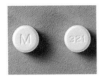

Lorazepam
0.5 mg tablet

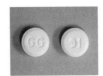

Lorazepam
0.5 mg tablet

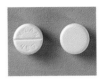

Lorazepam
1 mg tablet

Lorazepam
1 mg tablet

Lorazepam
1 mg tablet

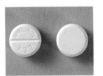

Lorazepam
2 mg tablet

Lorazepam
2 mg tablet

Nembutal
100 mg capsule

Oxazepam
10 mg capsule

Oxazepam
15 mg capsule

Oxazepam
20 mg capsule

Phenobarbital
15 mg tablet

Phenobarbital
16.2 mg tablet

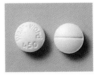

Phenobarbital
30 mg tablet

Phenobarbital
32.4 mg tablet

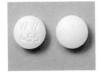

Phenobarbital
60 mg tablet

Phenobarbital
64.8 mg tablet

Phenobarbital
97.2 mg tablet

Phenobarbital
100 mg tablet

Prosom
1 mg tablet

Restoril
7.5 mg capsule

Restoril
15 mg capsule

Restoril
30 mg capsule

Seconal
100 mg capsule

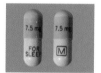

Temazepam
7.5 mg capsule

Temazepam
15 mg capsule

Temazepam
15 mg capsule

Temazepam
30 mg capsule

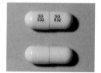

Temazepam
30 mg capsule

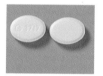

Triazolam
0.125 mg tablet

Triazolam
0.25 mg tablet

Valium
2 mg tablet

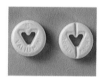

Valium
5 mg tablet

Valium
10 mg tablet

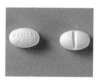

Xanax
0.25 mg tablet

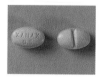

Xanax
0.5 mg tablet

Xanax
1 mg tablet

Xanax
2 mg tablet

Xanax XR
0.5 mg tablet

Xanax XR
1 mg tablet

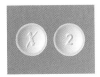

Xanax XR
2 mg tablet

Xanax XR
3 mg tablet

Appendix 4

Controlled Substance Act

Created along with the DEA in 1970, the Act lists all drugs with the potential for abuse by "Schedules" I through V, with I having the most potential for abuse and V the least. Schedule I drugs have no accepted medical use in the U.S. Manufacturing and distributing laws, prescribing and dispensing practices, as well as trafficking and possession laws correspond with the schedule of the drug.

President Nixon with Honorary DEA Agent Elvis Presley

Controlled Substance Schedules

Schedule I	Schedule II	Schedule III	Schedule IV	Schedule V
Heroin	Cocaine	Codeine	Benzodiazepines	
Methamphetamine		*(in combination drugs)*		
	Morphine	Buprenorphine	Propoxyphene	
LSD	Hydromorphone	Barbiturates		
Marijuana	Oxymorphone	Hydrocodone		
Psilocybin	Oxycodone	Ketamine		
Mescaline	Meperidine			
MDMA	Fentanyl			
PCP	Methadone			
	Amphetamine			
	Methylphenidate			
	Codeine			

Drug Use Time Table
(How Long Each Drug Stays in the Body)

Drug	Detection
Morphine	2-4 days
Codeine	2-4 days
Hydromorphone	2-4 days
Meperidine	2-4 days
Methadone	6-12 days
Hydrocodone	1-6 days
Oxycodone	8-24 hours
Barbiturates	2-10 days
Benzodiazepines	1-6 weeks
Cocaine	2-5 days
Amphetamines	1-2 days
Methylphenidate	1-2 days
Anorectics	1-2 days
LSD	8-24 hours
Mescaline	2-3 days
PCP	2-4 days
MDMA	2-5 days
Marijuana	2 days-11 weeks

Bibliography

The preparation of this book included numerous interviews with individuals receiving drug abuse treatment, many health care professionals involved in the delivery of drug abuse treatment, as well as the following list of articles, books and studies.

Pharmacology
Ballington, Don and Langden, Mary. *Pharmacology for Technicians.* Paradigm Publishing (2006)
Beaver County District Attorney's Office. *Drug Identification Guide.* (2008)
Hitner, Henry and Nagle, Barbara. *Pharmacology, An Introduction.* McGraw-Hill (2005)
Inaba, Darryl and Cohen, William and Holstein, Michael. *Uppers, Downers, All Arounders.* CNS
   Publications (1997)
Moini, Jahangir. Focus on Pharmacology, *Essentials for Health Professionals.* Pearson Prentice Hall (2008)
U.S. Dept of Justice, DEA. *Drugs of Abuse.* 2005 Edition
Wills, Simon. *Drugs of Abuse.* The Pharmaceutical Press (1987)

Opiates
"Codeine Information-Facts-Codeine" (http://codeine.50g.com/info/codeine)
"Methadone, Methadone Addiction & Methadone Side Effects By Narconon Arrowhead & Heroin
   Addiction" (HTML). http://www.heroinaddiction.com/heroin
"Opium Throughout History." PBS Frontline
   (http://www.pbs.org/wgbh/pages/frontline/shows/heroin)
"Oxycodone." Center for Substance Abuse Research. May 2, 2005.
   (http://www.cesar.umd.edu/cesar/drugs/oxycodone)
Acetaminophen side effects, drug class, medical uses, and drug interactions. MedicineNet.com
   (http://www.medicinenet.com/acetaminophen)
Anil Aggrawal. "Narcotic Drugs"(http://opioids.com/narcotic-drugs)
Booth, Martin. *Opium: A History.* London: Simon & Schuster, Ltd. (1996)
Budd K, Raffa RB (edts.) Buprenorphine: The unique opioid analgesic. Thieme (2005)

Clinical Guidelines for the Use of Buprenorphine in the Treatment of Opioid Addiction. Treatment Improvement Protocol(TIP) 40. Laura McNicholas. U.S. Dept of Health and Human Services

Codeine Information from Drugs.com (http://www.drugs.com/codeine)

DEA Briefs and Backgrounds, Drugs and Drug Abuse, Drug Descriptions, Narcotics (http://www.usdoj.gov/dea)

Demerol (http://www.rxlist.com/drugs)

Dilaudid Clinical Pharmacology (http://www.rxlist.com)

Drug Information Handbook. 13th ed. Hudson, OH (2005)

Drugs.com:Codeine Information. (http://www.drugs.com)

Gordon DB, Stevenson KK, Griffie J, et al. Opioid equianalgesic calculations. *J Palliat Med.* 1999;2(2):209-218

Heroin Information from the National Institute on Drug Abuse (http://www.nida.gov/infofacts/heroin)

http://www.erowid.org

Hydromorphone Consumer Drug Information (http://www.drugs.com/MTM/hydromorphone) *Drugs.com*

Inaba, Darryl and Cohen, William and Holstein, Michael. *Uppers, Downers, All Arounders*. CNS Publications (1997)

Joseph H., Stancliff S., Langrod J., "Methadone Maintenance Treatment (MMT): a review of historical and clinical issues." Mt. Sinai J Med. 67 (5-6):347-64

Komestsy, C. Action of opioid on the brain-reward system. In Rapaka, R.S. and Sorer, H; eds. Discovery of Novel Opiod Medications. National Institute on Drug Abuse Research Monograph 147 (1991)

Latta, Kenneth S; Brian Ginsberg, Robert L. Barkin (Jan/Feb 2002). "Meperidine: A Critical Review." *American Journal of Therapeutics* (Lippincott Williams & Wilkins)9(1):53-68

List of Scheduled Drugs, U.S. Department of Justice

McCoy, Alfred W. "Opium History, 1858 to 1940 (http://www.a1b2c3.com/drugs)

Methadone Pharmacokinetics-PubPK (http://www.pubpk.org)

Meyer, Jerrold S and Quenzer, Linda F. *Psychopharmacology. Drugs, The Brain And Behavior.* Sinauer Associates, Inc (2005)

Morphine withdrawal and depression (http://opioids.com.morphine)

Musto, David F., "Early History of Heroin in the United States," in P.G. Bourne, ed., Addiction (New York: Academic Press, 1974)

Musto, David F., The American Disease: Origins of Narcotic Control (New Haven: Yale University Press, 1973)

National Institute on Drug Abuse. "Heroin." *NIDA Capsule, NIDA* (1986)

NIDA InfoFacts on Heroin (http://www.nida.nih.gov/Infofacts/heroin)

Notes on heroin dosage and tolerance (http://www.erowid.org)

Office of National Drug Control Policy. Heroin Facts and Figures. Rockville, MD (2004)

SAMHSA (http://www.samhsa.gov)

Schmitz, Rudolf, "Friedrich Wilhelm Serturner and the Discovery of Morphine," Pharmacy in History 27 (1985)

Seidler, Raymond. "Prescription Drug Abuse." (July 2002) *Current Therapeutics. (http://www.nswrdn.com)*

The Ohio Resource Network for Safe & Drug Free Schools and Communities: www.ebasedprevention.org

U.S. DEA information: http://www.usdoj.gov/dea

Vallner JJ, Stewart JT, Kotzan JA, Kirsten EB, Honigberg IL. "Pharmacokinetics and bioavailability of hydromorphone following intravenous and oral administration." *J of Clinical Pharmacology* (1981) www.factsandcomparisons.com

Stimulants

Barnett G, Hawks R, Resnick R (1981). "Cocaine pharmacokinetics in humans." *J Ethnopharmacol* 3 (2-3):353-66.

Cocaine Drug Use and Dependence: Merck Manual Professional."

Cooper, DA. (1998), "Clandestine production processes for cocaine and heroin." United States Department of Justice Drug Enforcement Administration.

Drugs.com (2007-01-01). "Comnplete Khat Info." (http://www.drugs.com/npp/khat).

Drug Information Handbook.13th ed. Hudson, OH (2005)

Fone KC, McNutt DJ. (2005). "Stimulants: use and abuse in the treatment of attention deficit disorder." *Current opinion in pharmacology*. 5 (1):87-93.

Giannini AJ, Burge H, Shaheen JM, Price WA (1986). "Khat: another drug of abuse?." *J Psychoactive Drugs* 18 (2):155-8.

http://www.erowid.org

Kimko HC, Cross JT, Abernathy DR (1999). "Pharmacokinetics and clinical effectiveness of methylphenidate." *Clin Pharmacokinet* 37 (6):457-70.

List of Scheduled Drugs, U.S. Department of Justice

Lukas, SE. The Encylopedia of Psychoactive Drugs: Amphetamines. Chelsea House. (1985)

McGregor C, Srisurapanont M, Jittiwutikarn J, Laobhripatr S, Wongtan T, White J (2005). "The nature, time course and severity of methamphetamine withdrawal." *Addiction* 100 (9):1320-9.

Meyer, Jerrold S and Quenzer, Linda F. *Psychopharmacology. Drugs, The Brain And Behavior.* Sinauer Associates, Inc (2005)

Moore KE (1997), "The actions of amphetamine on neurotransmitters: a brief review." *Biol. Psychiatry* 12 (3):451-62.

NIDA research report series: Methamphetamine abuse and addiction (NIH Publication #06-4210, 2006)

NIDA. NIDA *InfoFacts,* Crack and Cocaine, 1998.

SAMHSA (http://www.samhsa.gov)

Schlesinger HL: Topics in the chemistry of cocaine; Bull Narc 37, 63 (1985).

Sulzer D, Sonders MS, Poulsen NW, Galli A (2005). "Mechanisms of neurotransmitter release by amphetamines: a review." *Prog Neurobiology*. 75 (6):406-33.

The Price and Purity of Illicit Drugs: 1981 Through the Second Quarter of 2003. (http://www.whitehousedrugpolicy.gov/publications/price)

U.S. DEA information: http://www.usdoj.gov/dea

U.S. Department of Justice, Drug Enforcement Administration, Office of Intelligence: Coca cultivation and cocaine processing: An overview; Arlington, VA (1993).

Volkow, ND, et al. Association of dopamine transporter reduction with psychomotor impairment in methamphetamine abusers. Am J Psychiatry 158(3):377-382. (2001)

Winslow BT, Voorhees KI, Pehl KA (2007). "Methamphetamine abuse." *American family physician* 76 (8):1169-74.

Wu LT, Pilowsky DJ, Schlenger WE, Galvin DM (2007). Misuse of methamphetamine and prescription stimulants among youths and young adults in the community. *Drug and Alcohol Dependence,* 89, 195-205.

www.factsandcomparisons.com

Depressants

American Psychiatric Association. *Benzodiazepine Dependence, Toxicity, and Abuse: A Task Force Report of the American Psychiatric Association.* Washington DC, (1990).

Ashton H. Benzodiazepine Abuse, Drugs and Dependence, Harwood Academic Publishers (2002), 197-212.

Ashton H. Benzodiazepine withdrawal: outcome in 50 patients. British Journal of Addiction (1987) 82, 662-671.

Cooper, Bloom and Roth. *The Biochemical Basis of Neuropharmacology.* Eaton T Forbes Research Center. (2002).

CSAT. *Detoxification from Alcohol and Other Drugs, Treatment Improvement Protocol* (TIP) #19. SAMHSA, (1985).

Harrison N, Mendelson WB, DeWit H (2000). "Barbiturates." Neuropsychopharmacology. ⟨http://www.acnp.org/g4⟩.

Hollister LE (1983). "The pre-benzodiazepine era." *J Psychoactive Drugs.* 15 (1-2):9-13.

Inaba, Darryl and Cohen, William and Holstein, Michael. *Uppers, Downers, All Arounders.* CNS Publications (1997)

Johns MW (1975). "Sleep and hypnotic drugs." Drugs 9 (6):448-78.

Littrell RA, Hayes LR, Stillner V. Carisoprodol (Soma): A new and cautious perspective on an old agent. *South Med J.* 1993;86(7):753-68.

Longo LP, Johnson B. Addiction:Part 1. Benzodiazepines-side effects, abuse risk, and alternatives. *American Family Physician* 61:2121-2131, (2000).

Meyer, Jerrold S and Quenzer, Linda F. *Psychopharmacology. Drugs, The Brain And Behavior.* Sinauer Associates, Inc (2005)

Reeves RR, Liberto V. Abuse of combinations of carisoprodol and tramadol. *South Med J.* 2001;94(5):512-14.

Hallucinogens

Abraham HD, Aldridge AM, Gogia P. The psychopharmacology of hallucinogens. *Neuropsychopharmacology* 14:285-298, (1986).

Adams IB, Martin BR. Cannabis: Pharmacology and toxicology in animals and humans. *Addiction* 91:1585-1614, (1996).

Aghajanian GK, Marek GJ. Serotonin and hallucinogens. *Neuropsychopharmacology* 21:16S-23S, (1999).

Bergman S (1999). "Ketamine: review of its pharmacology and its use in pediatric anesthesia." *Anesth Prog* 46 (1):10-20.

Breivogel CS, Scates SM, Beletskaya IO, Lowery OB, Aceto MD, Martin BR. The effecys of delta-9-THC physical dependence on brain cannabinoid receptors. *Euro J Pharmacology* 459:139-150 (2003)

Budney AJ, Moore BA, Vandrey RG, Hughes JR. The time course and significance of cannabis withdrawal. *J Abnorm Psych* 112 (3)393-402 (2003).

Calabrese JD. "The Therapeutic Use of Peyote in the Native American Church." *Psychedelic Medicine: New Evidence for Hallucinogens as Treatments.* Westport, CT: Praeger/Greenwood (2007)

Cohen S (Jan 1960). "Lysergic Acid Diethylamide: Side Effects and Complications." *J of Nerv Ment Dis* 130 (1):30-40.

Drug Enforcement Administration (May 2001). 2C-B *(Nexus) Reappears on the Club Drug Scene.* Press release.

ElSohly MA, Ross SA, Mehmedic Z, Arafat R, Yi B, Banahan B. Potency trends of delta-9-THC and other cannabinoids in confiscated marijuana from 1980-1997. *J Forensic Sci* 45 (1):24-30 (2000).

Erowid Ketamine Vault. (http//:www.erowid.org/chemicals/ketamine)

Giannini AJ. Drugs of Abuse, Second Edition. Los Angeles, Practice Management Information Corp, 1997.

Greer G, Tolbert R. "The Therapeutic Use of MDMA in Ecstasy: The clinical, pharmacological and neurotoxicological effects of the drug MDMA." 1990 (ed Peroutka SJ) Boston, p.21-36.

"InfoFacts-LSD." Nida.nih.gov. (2008-07-23).

"Information on Drugs of Abuse." *Commonly Abused Drug Chart.* (http://www.nida.nih.gov)

Liechti ME, Vollenweider FX. Which neuroreceptors mediate the subjective effects of MDMA inhumans? A summary of mechanistic studies. *Human Psychopharmacology* 16:589-598 (2001).

"LSD dangers." The Good Drug Guide. (http://www.thegooddrugguide.com)

"LSD Vault: Dosage." (http://www.erowid.org)

MAPS (http://www.maps.org/research)

NIDA. (2001). *Hallucinogens and dissociative drugs, including LSD, PCP, ketamine, dextromethorphan.* (DHHS Publication No. 01-4209).

Parrott AC, Lasky J. Ecstasy (MDMA) effect upon mood and cognition: before, during and after a Saturday night dance. *Psychopharmacology* 139:261-268 (1998).

Passie T, Seifert J, Schneider U, Emrich HM. (2002). "The pharmacology of psilocybin." *Addict. Biol.* 7 (4):357-64.

Strassman RJ (1984). "Adverse reactions to psychedelic drugs. A review of the literature." *J Nerv Ment Dis* 172 (10):577-95.

Walton RP. (1938). *Marijuana, America's New Drug Problem.* JB Lippincott. P.6.

Zakzanis KK, Campbell Z, Jovanovski D (Oct 2007). "The neuropsychology of ecstasy (MDMA) use; a quantitative review." *Hum Psychopharmacol* 22 (7):427-35.

Quick Order Form

Please visit our website at **www.drugsofabuse.net** to order books and to join the *Addiction Pharmacy* network.

You may also contact us at:

Three Suns Publishing
516 College Avenue
Beaver, Pa 15009
724-775-7921 (phone)
724-775-7921 (fax)
info@drugsofabuse.net